SAGE was founded in 1965 by Sara Miller McCune to support the dissemination of usable knowledge by publishing innovative and high-quality research and teaching content. Today, we publish over 900 journals, including those of more than 400 learned societies, more than 800 new books per year, and a growing range of library products including archives, data, case studies, reports, and video. SAGE remains majority-owned by our founder, and after Sara's lifetime will become owned by a charitable trust that secures our continued independence.

Los Angeles | London | New Delhi | Singapore | Washington DC | Melbourne

Praise for Walter Vieira's Earlier Books

[This book] should be read by all aspiring managers, as well as experienced managers, to get a picture of the real world of commerce and industry. Walter covers a wide spectrum of many practical questions and situations, that academicians generally ignore in their rarefied teaching.

A job seeker who is ready to enter the business world, needs to learn the ropes of job hunting, creating value, and moving up the ladder of management. The person needs a full understanding of the business challenges and opportunities he or she will face. Those in middle or senior management have other and sometimes more complex challenges, as they move towards the CEO position or toward retirement.

Let Walter be your guide, as you seek to enjoy a rich and rewarding career in management, with his central theme of high performance in tandem with high ethical standards.

—**Philip Kotler**

The author fills his work with many examples and anecdotes to ensure a painless read. [It is] a valuable read to win.
—*Business Line*

This is a book of difference. It tears the mask of management theory, which talks mainly about 'what should be', and shows instead 'what it is' that really happens in the workplace. It enables on to learn from other's experiences and not from one's own mistakes. Walter Vieira uses his enormous experience as a business consultant to present a step-by-step progression of corporate life and to provide lessons for shaping a successful corporate executive. Full of real-life examples and anecdotes, this book will enable managers to relate to, and tackle, everyday problems successfully.

—*Mid-Day, Delhi*

A guide meant for students of management and those working in the corporate sector, in this book the author uses his experience as a business consultant to present the reality, rather than just theoretical wisdom, pertaining to the corporate workplace.

—*The Tribune*

Providing practical advice and a sound foundation in sales management, the book helps sales managers revisit the theory of sales management in a simple, entertaining manner with the help of illustrations and real-life anecdotes.

—*The Asian Age*

A handy book, it is not limited to a purely western setting. With broken down narratives that are designed like short letters, there is a visual element that comes from cartoons and a design format for someone who may not be into reading lengthy passages. It also has typical examples drawn from small town Indian settings.

—*www.livemint.com*

With his vast experience as a corporate executive and a management consultant, Walter is best equipped to guide a rookie manager to produce his/her best in the corporate environs.

—*USP Age*

THE IMPATIENT MANAGER

Thank you for choosing a SAGE product!
If you have any comment, observation or feedback,
I would like to personally hear from you.

Please write to me at **contactceo@sagepub.in**

Vivek Mehra, Managing Director and CEO,
SAGE Publications India Pvt Ltd, New Delhi

Bulk Sales

SAGE India offers special discounts
for purchase of books in bulk.
We also make available special imprints
and excerpts from our books on demand.

For orders and enquiries, write to us at

Marketing Department
SAGE Publications India Pvt Ltd
B1/I-1, Mohan Cooperative Industrial Area
Mathura Road, Post Bag 7
New Delhi 110044, India

E-mail us at **marketing@sagepub.in**

Get to know more about SAGE

Be invited to SAGE events, get on our mailing list.
Write today to **marketing@sagepub.in**

This book is also available as an e-book.

THE IMPATIENT MANAGER

WALTER VIEIRA

Los Angeles | London | New Delhi
Singapore | Washington DC | Melbourne

Copyright © Walter Vieira, 2016

All rights reserved. No part of this book may be reproduced or utilized in any form or by any means, electronic or mechanical, including photocopying, recording or by any information storage or retrieval system, without permission in writing from the publisher. For the stories in the book, any resemblance to real persons, living or dead, is purely coincidental.

First published in 2016 by

SAGE Publications India Pvt Ltd
B1/I-1 Mohan Cooperative Industrial Area
Mathura Road, New Delhi 110 044, India
www.sagepub.in

SAGE Publications Inc
2455 Teller Road
Thousand Oaks, California 91320, USA

SAGE Publications Ltd
1 Oliver's Yard, 55 City Road
London EC1Y 1SP, United Kingdom

SAGE Publications Asia-Pacific Pte Ltd
3 Church Street
#10-04 Samsung Hub
Singapore 049483

Published by Vivek Mehra for SAGE Publications India Pvt Ltd, typeset in 11.5/14.5 pts ITC Century Book by Diligent Typesetter India Pvt Ltd, Delhi and printed at Sai Print-o-Pack, New Delhi.

Library of Congress Cataloging-in-Publication Data Available

ISBN: 978-93-859-8527-0 (PB)

The SAGE Team: Sachin Sharma, Kumar Indra Mishra, Neha Sharma and Ritu Chopra

*To my wife—Celine
and my children—Randhir, Samir, Latika,
and Priyanka
who are also Impatient Managers*

A Message for the Impatient Manager

Have the Courage to Succeed
To dream anything that you want to dream,
That's the beauty of the human mind.

To do anything that you want to do,
That is the strength of the human will.

To trust yourself to test your limits,
That is the courage to succeed
—Anonymous

Contents

Preface ix
Acknowledgments xi

1. A New World for the Young: The Balance Is Changing — 1
2. Be Positively Impatient: Look, Observe, Study, Implement — 21
3. Have a Vision: The Big Picture — 41
4. Be Innovative, Be Different: Understand Consumer Needs — 53
5. Add Width to Depth: Of Knowledge and Experience — 70
6. Go Beyond Technology: Add EQ and SQ to the IQ — 78
7. Build Networks: Most Often You Cannot Do It Alone — 99
8. Enthusiasm and Perseverance: Twin Engines of Success — 112
9. Managing Jealousy and Envy: Killers from the Inside — 127
10. Never Forget Those Who Helped You on the Way Up: A Way to Connect and Care — 137
11. Key Lessons in Leadership: A Changing Style for a New World — 148
12. The Corner Office Is Now Sometimes Temporary: So What Next? — 166

Epilogue 179
About the Author 183

Preface

The Impatient Manager would seem an unusual title for a book. The idea came from Sachin Sharma of SAGE, who after seeing the script of the revised edition of my book *Manager to CEO*, felt a great need to have a book for those who are not prepared to wait for twenty-five years of trials and tribulations to get to the corner office. *Manager to CEO* (SAGE) was written for the marathon race: starting from the bottom of the pyramid and working your way up to the top, which may take twenty or even thirty years.

But, there is the impatient manager of today; someone who wants to finish an MBA and become a CEO in eight to ten years or someone who starts as an entrepreneur and wants to be a CEO, founder, and a millionaire in five years. There are many role models, especially in the latter category, such as founders of Flipkart, Snapdeal, Quickr, Jabong, Myntra, CarTrade, Housing.com, Uber, Ola, and thousands of others, from the earlier one, Hotmail's founder Sabir Bhatia.

In fact, seventy-two percent of the startups in India, in the last three years, have been by entrepreneurs below thirty-five years of age. The average age of startup founders is twenty-eight, and three to four startups are born every day. The estimated funding for startups in 2015 alone was $5 billion. And about 85,000 people are employed in the startups.

"What man has done, man can do" and "The glory is in the striving, not in the attaining." These are often repeated quotes. And very true! So, why not try? This is why I wrote this book.

As a quick read of less than 200 pages, it can be read in a sitting of two to three hours. The book cannot provide any complete solution; however, it can act as a cautionary *road sign* when you are driving at 130 mph over a winding path to the top. It will help you out in avoiding the oncoming traffic or overtaking traffic so that you would not get derailed. With a constant high speed, you should be able to reach the top in a short period (whatever this period may be).

With twelve short pieces of advice from people who have influenced me, as well as some of my own, I wish the "impatient managers" all success. Throughout this book I have referred to "he"—which also includes "she"—only for the simplicity of the writing.

Perhaps, I can also add, tongue in cheek,
If you want to avoid high traffic, try taking the road to success!

—**Walter Vieira**

Acknowledgments

My grateful thanks to the following highly eminent personalities of India, who are role models for the new generation of entrepreneurs and corporate managers, for sharing their experiences and thoughts and taking out time to write messages to the young Impatient Managers. This is greatly appreciated.

Mr Adi Godrej	Chairman, Godrej Industries Ltd. and Former President, Confederation of Indian Industry (CII)
Mr Anil Khandelwal	Former Chairman and Managing Director, Bank of Baroda
Mr Habil Khorakiwala	Chairman, Wockhardt Ltd., India
Mr Harsh Mariwala	Chairman, Marico Ltd.
Mr Keki Mistry	Managing Director, HDFC Ltd., India
Mr Harish Mehta	Managing Director, Onward Technologies, India and Ex-chairman/Co-founder, NASSCOM, India
Ms Kiran Mazumdar Shaw	Chairman and Managing Director, Biocon Ltd., India

1

A New World for the Young
The Balance Is Changing

TIME OF GREAT CHANGE

It is a time of great change. Of course, every century has been a period of change. But last fifty years, that has been the period of my working life, has shocked all of us with the "speed of change." Earlier, it was the printing press that had a great impact on the world. The next landmarks were the chip and computer. Now the digital media has taken knowledge and information to some of the remotest areas of the world. In India, many people, even in villages which do not have road access or do not have sanitation and safe drinking water, have a "mobile". They are connected; they know what is going on in the rest of the world, which creates both "inspiration" and "aspirations". Many of them also want to get to the world that they see on the smartphone and on the television.

"UP boy hopes to live his Indian Institute of Technology Bombay (IIT-B) dream with sister's old laptop" was a headline in a newspaper of July 24, 2015. It was accompanied by a photograph of Anshu Ahirwar and his father, sitting on the steps of the IIT-B. Anshu belongs to a very poor family in Uttar Pradesh. His father is a daily wage mason in the small town of Orai and is the sole bread winner for a family of four children. Anshu scored 91.2

percent in Class XII and got admission into IIT-B, where he had to pay ₹78,000 (approx. $1,300) for college admission and accommodation fees. He was trying for loans and scholarships, and hoped he would succeed. He wanted to do Computer Science, and was sure he would succeed. His only weapon then was an old computer which he had borrowed from his sister, who got it as a prize when she excelled in her own examination some years ago.

There is so much of "inspiration" and "aspirations" in the new economy and new environment.

GENERATION Y PREFERS NEW-AGE CAREERS

Another news report in August 2015 stated that at least seventy-five percent of students prefer to go in for new-age careers over traditional careers. Apparently, the survey was done among 5,000 students in the age group of fifteen to twenty-one across seventy-five different cities by CareerGuide.com and shared with *Economics Times*, India.

Now the question is: what are the new age careers? Strangely, some of them are content writing, psychology, travel and tourism, biotechnology, digital marketing, and graphic designing. In the metro cities, careers such as social work and nonprofits are emerging as popular segments. On the other hand, teaching, civil services, medical, and information technology are more popular among rural youth, while management and marketing, economics, travel and tourism are more popular among the urban youth. In tier 2 and tier 3 cities, B.Com. and B.A. courses are popular, whereas in the metros, people seek industry-oriented training.

ARRIVE THE IMPATIENT MANAGER

Now, we see the impatient manager, whether a corporate executive or an entrepreneur, a young man or woman belonging to the post-2010 era, who is a person in a hurry—in a hurry to get to the finish and to get there fast. He wants to run the 100-meter race and finish it; then run the next 100 meters, and perhaps repeat the run, again and again. The days of running the long marathon are over.

Those were the days when I started out in the mid-1960s, to join as a management trainee in a large multinational, Glaxo, with dreams of heading it as CEO, after perhaps twenty years and, thus, spending a period of thirty years in the company. In those days, one only dreamt about the marathon.

I am reminded of the new-gen sprint king, Usain Bolt, who is now preparing himself for his fourth successive world title in the 200 meters. Bolt is the winner of an astonishing ten of the last eleven individual Olympic and world sprint titles since shooting to fame at the 2008 Beijing Olympic games. Bolt is a new-gen phenomenon!

YOUNG IN YEARS, HIGH IN REMUNERATION

A report in the *Times of India* on July 20, 2015, about Hindustan Unilever Limited (HUL), headlined, "HUL Fast Minting Crorepatis Group." The report talks about HUL's million dollar salary club. It offers eight-digit salaries to 169 managers, with eighty-eight managers below forty years of age and thirty-one managers below thirty-five years.

These 169 managers, who represent just one percent of HULs' total workforce, take home a combined salary of ₹310 crores (over $54 million). It is way more than the total employee spend of midsize companies like Marico, Godrej Consumer, and P&G Hygiene and Healthcare.

The HUL number is also fifty-six percent higher than IT major, Infosys, which has 123 eight-digit salary earners and more than double of seventy such salary earners in Wipro. No wonder HUL has been able to retain top class talent for much longer periods of time. HUL is often referred to as a CEO factory, having contributed over 400 CEOs to the corporate world.

Each company will have to work out for itself; its own justification for the very wide gap between the highest and the lowest salaries within the same organization. It will always remain a contentious issue and open to debate.

OLD EMPLOYEES LIKE YOUNG BOSSES

It was always assumed that the older employees will resent having to report to younger bosses—sometimes, so much younger, that they could have been the age of their children. However, there is also the surprising factor that, now, over sixty percent of employees in India prefer a young boss over an older and more experienced one.[1] Specifically in the new IT sector, seventy-five percent of the employees prefer a young boss while sixty-three percent employees in other sectors prefer a young boss. Only with senior professionals with over twenty years of experience, the preference is eighty percent for older bosses, and this is understandable.

Employees find young bosses to be understanding, more practical in solving problems, and friendly.

So the old barriers to young bosses no longer exist.

---

[1] A study by TimesJobs.com. Survey conducted on 650 employees in July 2015.

MORE ROOM AT THE TOP

The redrafted Companies Act, 2014, in India, has now set the ceiling of seventy years for all executive positions, even if the executive is a major shareholder in the enterprise. Special permission will have to be sought from the Company Law Board by those who want to stay on and permissions are being sought by a few, the likes of Azim Premji of Wipro (who is seventy-two) and others like PRS Oberoi of Oberoi Hotels (who is eighty-six) and many in between like Rahul Bajaj (at seventy-seven). There are still those who argue that as long as the person can deliver and add value to the organization, age should not matter. It should be left to the board to decide and later the shareholders to approve or reject.

Since there is now a regulation, there will be more room at the top.

BILLION DOLLAR BABIES BECKON

There are billion dollar babies beckoning to us and showing us the new direction in which the world is moving. The media recently listed the six youngest billionaires in the world, all below the age of thirty-one with a worth of over $1.5 billion.

- Evan Spiegel (twenty-five) the cofounder of Snapchat with 100 million users every month ($1.5 billion).
- Bobby Murphy (twenty-six) also a cofounder of Snapchat ($1.5 billion).
- Wang Han (twenty-seven) of Juneyao Airlines Company in Shanghai ($1.5 billion).
- Julio Mario Santo Domingo III (twenty-nine) the disc jockey in New York ($2.2 billion).

- Mark Zuckerberg (thirty-one) who created Facebook ($33.4 billion).
- Elizabeth Holmes (thirty-one) the youngest self-made woman billionaire and founder of Theranos, the blood testing company ($4.5 billion).

CORPORATES PROMOTE INTRAPRENEURS

There are now many companies that really promote "intrapreneurship." It gives enterprising staff a chance to participate in wealth creation. These companies realize that the brighter and more educated types want to do things on their own. So they can now be allowed to invest, perhaps to have sweat equity and, therefore, a sense of ownership.

Cisco and Mondelez have entrepreneurs—who are also their employees—who invest their own capital in startups they are building within the company. Mahindra is starting a similar program—where each startup will be a separate legal entity with a separate shareholding pattern and Mahindra and Mahindra will become an investor in these along with other investors.

This is something that one would never have thought of, perhaps, even ten years ago. If you had the "entrepreneur bug," you just quit and go on your own without bothering about the consequences. The new dispensation enables you to be a risk taker in a very limited way while still being shielded by a corporate umbrella.

It is a changing world of opportunities for the young, thus, helping to create *The Impatient Manager*.

Even startups are promoting "intrapreneurship." It is not only the old, established, and enlightened companies like Mondelez and Cisco, but also the young startup companies that promote intrapreneurship.

Ambarish Gupta, founder of Knowlarity—a cloud telephony company—took Chaudhary and Kohli—his employees—under his wing when he found that they wanted to start on their own. Gupta helped them start Cook Gourmet.

For the employee–entrepreneur, this degree of maturity is a "God-send" in a high mortality industry. Most of the times, the mentors (like Gupta) may not even claim stakes in the new venture. But the intrapreneur gets experienced mentoring and easier access to investors because of his past background and connections.

There are role models, of course, like Microsoft Garage, a platform for employees to ideate after hours on projects they may have in mind, and InMobi, which has a dedicated space for employees to work on unrelated projects. Surprising, but true!

PERMANENT JOBS ARE PASSÉ

HR experts predict that employees will soon be attracted by assignments, and not by jobs, perks, or the designation. They have confidence that the demand will be much more than the supply of their kind of services, so they can charge more. Yet, the company will find it economical because it does not have a fixed overhead.

They see a future where people know that even temporary jobs can be permanent and permanent jobs can be temporary. So we have situations where employees, so called, are working with as many as three different companies simultaneously.

They, now, call them "interim executives" in the West—they work on defined projects for just a few weeks or even a few months. They become tantamount to "consultants" and this trend is going to hurt the consulting industry. But again, we have to think of it as a part of the "time of change."

CHANGING TIMES!

We always get aware of the new professions that are emerging in the new environment. There are opportunities in the IT sector, ITES sector, BPOs, tourism and hospitality industry, financial sector, the infrastructure, biotechnology, solar energy, and many others. However, we also need to sit back and think about the many careers that have disappeared in the new economy. New technology and the pressure for new ways of doing things have made many professions redundant. Therefore, young people today must be constantly aware of which professions are going to disappear in the near future and what are the upcoming, or existing, but growth areas.

There was a time when my cousin earned a lot of money as a "navigator" for an international airline for close to fifteen years. And then, the airplanes were designed to do without a navigator and the job no longer exists. He had to go away and take up farming in Nashik. Fortunately, he had a positive attitude. He did not sit at home and mope, cursing his bad luck.

We always used travel agents to book our airline tickets and do our hotel bookings. It's not needed anymore. Now, using the internet, we can log in to travel websites, such as makemytrip.com or cleartrip.com or the website of the airline itself, and book our tickets at the best price available from among competitive airlines, perhaps, using TripAdvisor. It is same with hotels as well. One can specify the area in the city where the hotel should be, know the prices of competitive hotels, and complete the booking online using a credit card. Over the internet, one can see the hotel, the hotel rooms, the facilities offered, and every other detail. Often a travel agent cannot give you so much of information. So, goodbye travel agents!

We also needed a stock broker to buy and sell stock at regular intervals. We do not need to do this anymore. Many banks, such as ICICI and HDFC, offer facilities for stock trading over the internet. You can buy and sell whenever you like in the comfort of your home or office, which means, goodbye to stock brokers!

Bank clerk was a much sought after occupation. The jobs were well-paid and offered lifetime employment, security guaranteed by trade unions, and promotions at regular intervals in the public sector banks. The introduction of computers has changed it all. That is why bank workers unions resisted computerization for a long time. One computer can do the job of many, perhaps ten clerks. No longer will there be crowds waiting for the selection interview at banks for this, once valued assignment.

The road sweepers job with the Mumbai Municipal Corporation was a valued job because of the free quarters provided, security in service, and preference to children of municipal workers for the job. When I see the new road sweeping machines operating in some areas of the city, I know that "times" are changing!

Stenographers from Davers or Burnleys in Mumbai—a qualification which guaranteed jobs thirty years ago. Many were recruited from these institutions as soon as they had finished their program. There are no stenos anymore. They have metamorphosed into personal assistants who use computers. And the boss handles much of the correspondence on his own laptop anyway.

During my young days, there were eight laundries in my neighborhood. Today there are two. People use wash and dry fabrics, they use wrinkle free fabric, they have washing machines at home, and they have need only to get their silks and woolen suits dry cleaned some of the time. The laundry business has contracted though, perhaps, it will never shut down.

Young people must see the signs of the changing times and the beacons of the future. Those who do will succeed. Those who do not will be left on the banks of a fast flowing river.

WITHSTANDING PRESSURES RE CAREERS

One of the ten rules for a success in life, propounded by Cyrus Vance—author of *Manager Today, Executive Tomorrow*—is "progress means different things to different people." Do not use the achievements of others to measure your own success. Each of us needs to set our own goals, based on our capacity and capability. And then we have to measure ourselves against these goals. Each one is called to play a different role. If we play this well, to the best of our ability, we would not just be happy but contented; doing what we like to do rather than doing what we have to do.

I was, therefore, distressed to read a headline in the *Times of India* of December 11, 2012, "IITians struggle to live up to families' fat package dreams." A student of civil engineering confesses that four years ago when he qualified in the JEE, his family members were thrilled and shared their joy that he would soon be earning in dollars. The pressure to live by their expectations is constantly weighing on him. It would seem that enough is never enough.

Another student, who had just cleared the JEE, wanted to do aeronautical engineering. But his ambitious and enthusiastic father did a quick survey of all the IIT departments and was put off by the average salaries offered to past students of aeronautical engineering—poor compared to other departments. So he pushed his son into doing electrical engineering. Who knows, we might have lost an outstanding aeronautical engineer for an average electrical engineer! There are many presumptions that mislead parents and students, such as

- Every IITian gets multiple offers and is spoilt for choice.
- Every IITian gets a choice of Rupee and dollar salaries.
- Every IITian has a choice of working abroad.
- Only technical skills and exam performance will bag them the best jobs.
- The highest salary—received by one or two—of ₹60–80 lakhs per annum is the average salary offered.

None of the above is true. It is only a few that may have the options. Others have to accept local jobs at ₹8–11 lakhs per annum and be happy that they are gainfully employed.

Unfortunately, the setting of wrong and unrealistic goalposts does not end with the first placement. A Vice President of one of the large companies of a conglomerate in India applied for the position of President of a midsized company. I asked him why he wanted to change even though he was happy in his job, had climbed the ladder steadily over twenty years, was not unhappy with his company or the boss, and was paid adequately by market standards. The answer was: "Most of my batch mates from the class of 1985 have become Presidents, I am still a VP." I convinced him to stay where he was and use his own measure of progress. He stayed to later become the President of the same large conglomerate.

Progress means different things to different people. But if you do something useful, make a contribution, and have the passion for what you do you will achieve the contentment which money alone can never buy. For example, Nikhesh Arora is a CEO, founder, and serial entrepreneur, who is among the most high profile investors in the e-commerce area in India.

In a media note, in *Times of India* in October 2015, he says that when he completed his bachelor's degree, he badly wanted to work in the entertainment industry in Bollywood. He had a couple of high paying job offers, but he chose to take a lower paying job, which was in a different role. But it was a job in the right industry, at least, for him.

It was with Miramax Films. This job gave him exposure to films like Reservoir Dogs and Pulp fiction; far broader and deeper than he could ever have imagined. It opened a world of opportunities for him later on, and now, he is where he is—close to the pinnacle of achievement—not just in terms of money but in self-satisfaction.

Arora is now the President and apparent heir of Softbank, a $92 billion Japanese telecom and internet giant, led by Masayachi Som, the richest man in Japan. Som says that India is a top priority for Softbank. They intend to invest nearly $10 billion in India over the next few years, mainly in Indian e-tail and technology companies. (Softbank has already invested $20 million in Chinese e-commerce giant Alibaba in 2000). Softbank is leading a $650 million financing round in Snapdeal, and pumping in $180 million in Ola, the taxi handling setup. Besides a joint venture with Bharti Telecom, it has also invested in the mobile advertising network, InMobi. Softbank is the lead company in investing $20 billion in solar energy projects in India with Bharti and Foxcom of Taiwan as minor partners. And Nikesh Arora is at the center of all this frenetic activity.

PEER GROUP PRESSURES

It has never been as much in the past as it is now. And, perhaps, it will be even more in the future. Here we are talking about the peer pressure on an individual of a peer group. If you do not fall in line with the group, you could get isolated, left out, considered a quirk, a stick in the mud, and "not one of us."

That is how a young person gets initiated into smoking to be one of the boys, or drinking alcohol till one is totally drunk and unstable "to be one of the girls," or taking to "ecstasy" to be "one of the hep crowds."

In Mumbai, we have had so many examples in the recent years. Taking the example of a young man, who packed his car with friends after a drunken party and drove recklessly down the seaside promenade late in the night to finally drive over some laborers sleeping on the pavement, killing some, and injuring the others. A few in the car were not drunk at all, but they were "part of the group." And they got implicated.

There was a big party at a beachside restobar, which was raided by the police. And most of the young people, coming from wealthy families, were arrested and tested positive for "drugs." There were also some people who claimed that they did not partake, but they got implicated because they were part of the group. Peer pressure had brought them here and there was only trouble at the end of the tunnel.

The first value in Cyrus Vance's book, *Manager Today, Executive Tomorrow*, is "you are alone" in life. You are really the master of your own destiny; you can make or break. You may have parents to help you on in the early part of the life and friends, classmates, and teachers later in the life. Even later, there may be the spouse and perhaps children. They are all there as companions and as a resource, for some of the times, at different times in life. No one in your entire life can really help you except as a temporary "aide". The reality is that all the time we are all alone.

We must, therefore, strike our own path and clear the way to create that path. No one else can do this for us. You are alone! We all are. Finding solutions in "group movement" to identify your life's goals is a dream, a chimera. You have to write your own life script. And the script is different for every individual.

But, if you can be with the crowd and yet not a part of it, if you can stand aside with your own beliefs, goals, and time schedules to achieve them, you will win in the long run. There may be transient embarrassments and even jeering. But if you know where you are going, it will not matter. You will get there. Many of them may not.

It's like the motorist who whizzed past you by overtaking from the left, then zipped through traffic changing lanes and going beyond speed limits and who you see meeting with an accident further down the road. You are not glad it happened, but it did. And you keep driving along at a steady pace, following the rule book, finally to reach your destination.

TALENT AND CAREERS 2015 ONWARD

As I look forty years back in the 1960s when only limited opportunities existed, I often feel envious of those who live in the present time, the 2000s. Forty years ago, the accepted professions were doctor, engineer, and lawyer and there was a section that thought about government service such as the Indian Administrative Service, Indian Police Service, Indian Audit and Account Service, Indian Revenue Service, and finally the Indian Forest Service. These were careers, the former, with a potential for great wealth and respect if successful or the latter with great power and status even if they were not highly efficient, or deliver results.

All this is past. The future belongs to those who want to do what they like and like what they do.

If you really like what you do, and that is your job for a living, then you will never have to work a day in your life. Because your hobby is your work and your work is your hobby.

No longer do we need to meet our parents' expectations for "security" by embarking on a "standard" profession or their demands for "continuity"—to become a lawyer because the father is a lawyer or join the civil service because the father was in the IAS.

In the 2000s, your "talent" and "inclination" lead you to a "career". You can make a career out of every talent and you can keep changing careers when you are bored, tired of routine, need an outlet for new innovations, or if you have other talents.

When you look around, there are many examples such as the son of K.M. Birla, who dreams of becoming a soccer star and is working toward this, or the son of

Ivan Fernandez, an IT czar in Dubai, whose son is training for golf championships in an academy in Florida and doing the circuit.

Money has ceased to be the main motivator in deciding a career. Sure, money is important but up to a point, no further. Beyond that, self-satisfaction or self-actualization is more important. If there is talent and the job satisfaction, it is assumed that the money will follow. And if it does not follow in a flood, there will, at least, be a regular flow. You will never be in need and you will be healthy because you are happy.

We are in an age which is also marked by new boundaries and new unwritten rules. Some of these rules are:

- People now look for "assignments, not careers." Very few young people now think about a lifelong career with a company.
- People now have a "different set of loyalties." In the past, the first loyalty was to the boss now it is to yourself.
- Every "pursuit" could be "for the time being." At the "plateau", people think about "what next" and then take a different road when they come to the fork in the road.
- "Social approval," which was paramount in the past, does not seem to matter as much now. Self-satisfaction is paramount; social or community approval is subsidiary.

However, it brings in a lot of responsibility for the young person. He must know his strengths and weaknesses and understand the opportunities and threats. It is SWOT (strengths, weaknesses, opportunities, and threats). Those, who know themselves well and can understand the environment, are the ones who will finally win the career battles of the 2000s.

> **Case Study**
>
> A young man was fond of hair styling. He went to France to gain the specialization. He returned to India and started a hairdressing salon in Colaba, Mumbai. Many friends of his parents were shocked and some dismayed, especially since, Miranda Sr., the father, was a well-known cartoonist. But the salon did excellently. It was a one week wait for appointments. Today the young man is using his artistic scissors in New York. He has both job satisfaction and money. It was the beginning of a very successful career. He does not seem to be working a single day of his life.
>
> He has not built a big empire and, perhaps, never will. But it does not matter.

THE COMPANY WE KEEP: INFLUENCERS

Even though we may not be conscious of it, most of us are subtly influenced by the company we keep. This is why so many parents are paranoid about which schools their children should attend. It is not just the quality of teaching, the school curriculum—which, in many cases, is standard—or even the convenience of the location, but the kind of students that the children will mix, study, and play with. It is the "class" of the students who will, perhaps, be friends for life. The old "school tie" club!

In many cases, it has worked out in the "school tie" fashion. Rajiv Gandhi filled his kitchen cabinet with his old Doon School pals, like the two Aruns—Singh and Nehru. In better times, Vijay Mallya remained loyal to some of his Kolkata school pals, many of whom found some corner in the then growing UB empire.

Many of us are influenced by our friends in the kind of careers we choose. Because some of our friends are single-mindedly pursuing the goal of getting into an Indian Institute of Technology, we do the same. Avinash, who was thus influenced, ended up getting a lower rank in the IIT list and was offered—not mechanical, electronic, or electrical engineering—admission to Bachelors in Metallurgy. He accepted this because he wanted the IIT label. Actually, he had not the slightest interest in Metallurgy. Like many of his IIT classmates, Avinash also migrated to the USA and now works for a software firm where he does not use any of the knowledge he acquired at the B.Met program at IIT Mumbai. Had he done a program in software or in computer sciences, it would have been much more relevant.

A far more important and useful area of influence, by friends in school or college, is really in "attitudes and values" rather than imitation in courses and expertise. Do we have friends, who influence us in the use of drugs, alcohol, smoking, or fast driving?

However, peer pressure can also work the other way round. When I was in college, a fellow student, though senior, Peter Sinai, had graduated and was preparing for the civil services exams. He took it very seriously. He had set his heart on the IFS and for a whole year, he prepared for the same, working twelve hours a day. There were no movies, no parties, and no picnics for a whole year. The relaxation was long walks, as an evening outing.

He allowed no distractions. And when the results were released, he had stood first both at the IAS and the IFS. This attitude and sense of priorities and values left a lasting impression on many of his friends and on me as well.

Peter Sinai later became India's Ambassador to Sri Lanka. Earlier, he was posted at Moscow and Washington and had a distinguished career.

The lesson from this is clear. Use the concept of learning values and attitudes from friends and colleagues. There is no need for blind imitation of careers and goals. Others' goals, however lofty, may not be suitable for you. But others' lofty values and attitudes can be adopted with benefit to help achieve your own goals. Understand that change is taking place all the time all around you; you must welcome it and respond to it.

A Message from a Leader

The advice I would like to give the young leaders is that whether you decide to become an entrepreneur or work for an organization, you need to set your goals early in life. You need to ensure that your goals reflect your passion and not your fears. Do not fall into the trap of mimicking other people's choices, but educate yourself on the different career options, so as to choose the right path for yourself.

But once you set your goals, do not waver from that path. It is true that you will face many obstacles, but patience and perseverance will be the key to your success. Stick to your beliefs and pursue a course of action even in the face of overwhelming criticism and great adversity.

Along your journey, there will be many things that will entice you toward them, but do not get distracted. There are no shortcuts to success. Ensure that you do not get attracted to the false lure of greed. Success is attained by a single minded devotion wherein the core values must be unshakeable. As it is aptly said "integrity is not a 90 percent thing or a 95 percent thing; either you have it or you don't."

Remember that the road is long and winding in parts, and it is important to keep the long-term picture in mind. In life, sometimes, you will be ahead of the curve and sometimes behind. Do not let failure bog you down and never let yesterday's disappointments overshadow tomorrows dreams. Always remember that life is a marathon and not a sprint, and you will have sufficient time to turn things around.

Finally, you can't rest on your laurels and be on a self-congratulatory mode. You need to show humility and never stop learning at every stage of your life.

Keki Mistry
Managing Director, HDFC Ltd., India

2

Be Positively Impatient
Look, Observe, Study, Implement

"Ability is what you are capable of doing. Motivation determines what to do. Attitude determines how well you do it."

—**Aldous Huxley**

Those in a hurry, while driving, are likely to ignore traffic signals or ignore other traffic or, perhaps, meet with an accident or find themselves only just ahead of the cars they have overtaken at the next traffic light, or find themselves noticed on the radar and presented with a traffic violation ticket.

It is the same with the road to the top—the road to success!

Therefore, it is necessary to "hurry slowly" but "hurry nevertheless."

However, there should be some CAUTIONS.

- *See*: Do not just LOOK! Many people look but do not see. Like the car driver in his anxiety to reach the destination does not really see the traffic on the sides.
- *Observe*: Use judgment to decide when the lights will change, what the volume of traffic is, the impact of heavy rains, pot holed roads, and diversions of the traffic.

- *Study*: What are the advantages and disadvantages of alternate courses of action? What is the impact—short-term, mid-term, and long-term? With all the facts available at the time, is this the best decision you can take? Moreover, take the decision on time. The right decision at the wrong (delayed) time is a wrong decision.
- *Implement*: Many times there is a huge gap between planning and implementing. When that happens, there is failure. Try to match the "plan" derived after seeing, observing, and studying—with the ability to "implement" it. It is a major problem in most of the situations—where there are good intentions, but it never happens.

Case Study

Vasant Narkar (late) was born in a village near Ratnagiri (Western India) into a poor family. He walked eight kilometers to school, come rain or shine. Later, his uncle who stayed near to the school offered to host Vasant provided he did all the housework after school hours. Vasant did brilliantly at the High School Exams and went to Mumbai where he got a job as a typist clerk in a chartered accountant's firm. He did his B.Com, attending morning classes for four years and stood among the top ten. The CA firm made an exception with Vasant, and allowed him to hold his job (since he needed the income) while doing his Articles. Again, at the CA exams, Vasant excelled. Much later, he started his own CA Company, Narkar & Associates, and was invited to be on the board of directors of prestigious multinationals like Boots & E Merck. Unfortunately, he died in his sixties but left a shining example of See, Observe, Study, and Implement (SOSI). Vasant knew where he was going, planned to get there, and finally, got there.

Case Study

Surinder came as a refugee from Pakistan to Bombay with just a High School Certificate and lived in one of the refugee camps in Ulhasnagar, a distant suburb of Bombay. He quickly learned typing and joined a multinational as a typist clerk. Having then found stenos were better paid; he learned shorthand and was promoted. By the dint of hard work, by going beyond the job, and blessed with a photographic memory, Surinder moved on to junior manager in purchase, to sales manager, marketing director, and then to managing director, all in a space of fifteen years, leaving many better "qualified" contenders in the race far behind. I remember Surinder telling me, "I had decided that I will move from Ulhasnagar Camp to Malabar Hill (the home of the crème de la crème in Bombay) as soon as possible, and I will work toward achieving this." He did it in just fifteen years.

Surinder had a vision, knew his capabilities and capacity, his strengths and weaknesses, and he added large dollops of hard work and achieved his goals.

NINE TIPS FROM CATHY (ADAPTED)

Cathy Han, founder of 42 (Y Combinator W14), a data analytics company, has this advice to give a young first-time startup CEO.

1. *Have DETERMINATION.* It is the biggest predictor of long-term success. Nobody has an easy road. Remember Edison and the 10,000 experiments he had to do before succeeding with the electric bulb?
2. *You will grow by what you MEASURE.* Have weekly goals with metrics such as number of users or revenues. Be specific!
3. *Do not mistake ACTIVITY for GROWTH.* Adding customers and building product sales is the only real growth. Everything else is just activity and counts for little in final success. Peter Drucker was right when he kept repeating that "the only two revenue centers in the company are innovation and marketing; all the rest are costs."
4. *Constantly MOVE FORWARD.* More product benefits, more outlets, more geographical area, more customers, more repeat customers, less outstandings/debts.
5. *Play on your STRENGTHS.* No one is good at everything. The winner between the alligator and the bear is determined by the terrain. So understand your strengths and then play on them.
6. *Make DECISIONS FAST.* Remember there are only twenty-four hours in a day and only about ten percent of the information is really needed to make most of the decisions. Train yourself to become

decisive, so that you can move forward with the execution.
7. *Do not focus too much on the COMPETITION.* Stay aware of the players in the space you are in, but focus on getting to the top of your game. In any case, what others are doing is out of your control.
8. *There is no substitute for HARD WORK.* The good news is that the tougher it is for you, the more difficult it is for others to replicate.
9. *OPPORTUNITY is everywhere.* Therefore, there is no end to innovation that is possible. Think of all the "unicorns" (founders of startups with billion dollar valuations) like Kunal Bahl of Snapdeal, Bhavish Aggarwal of Ola, Pranay Chulet of Quikr, Naveen Tewari of InMobi's, Vijay Sekhar Sharma of PayTM, and others. They are all innovators "par excellence."

CHANCE MEETINGS

- In only the last few months, I read about a young man at IIT-B (Bombay) Incubation Centre. He had developed an "app" which can be used by passengers to check a "tampered taxi meter" and know whether he is being cheated.

In an environment where cab drivers invariably take "customers for a ride," it is an invaluable aid to fight the evil of tampered taxi meters.

- Another young man that I met at the Agnel Technical Incubation Centre, Goa had developed a water purifier which can be connected to a mechanical water hand pump and can give clear and clean potable water even in the remotest village of India which has no electricity. That too, at a very low price.

Is it not amazing what young people can think of, and do things to make it a better world.

STARTUPS ARE FORCING ESTABLISHED COMPANIES TO CHANGE FOR THE BETTER

One would have expected the old and large companies to be fighting the new startups which are "johnny-come-lately." But there are some companies that see the writing on the wall and have been proactive, not just reactive.

PRS Oberoi, Chairman of the Oberoi group, says that they always encourage managers to treat the business as their own. He says that there are, at least, ten former executives of Oberoi who have built businesses of some significance with the help and support of the company. They are not direct competitors even now and they continue to be friends.

Harsh Mariwala, Chairman of Marico, says that they have to be in constant search of new ideas across processes. And there is a high need to establish network outside your traditional community. He admits that he has picked up a lot of learning from his personal investments in startups.

Anand Mahindra of M&M says that betting on people and ideas has become a way of life.

Thus, even well-established companies are inadvertently opening doors for the nimble footed entrepreneur who has the passion and the drive to make it happen.

NIMBLE-FOOTED ENTREPRENEURS

We live in a time when one can change a career in early life or even midlife as circumstances dictate. Those with a positive attitude, who believed in looking forward and building rather than looking back at the wreckage, were those who generally succeeded.

There are also those of a different breed—the self-employed, the entrepreneurs. They have to think on their feet, and more speedily in a world that is changing fast. And most of the intrepid, self-motivated entrepreneurs are very adept at this; far more adept than the large corporations, the behemoths who find it difficult to move. Who cannot be as nimble because of their size. In spite of what Rosabeth Moss Kanter may say in her book *When Elephants Learn to Dance*. Very few elephants do learn. Most mice find their way in, even past firmly closed doors.

Case Study

Carl P finished a course in Cost Accounting and got into business with some partners in poultry farming. After a successful run, the partnership had problems and he took his share and went into the printing business. When margins in the printing business began to thin, he began a partnership to make ice cream cones. He then moved into screen printed hoarding sheets until Chinese machines came into the country and upset existing economics in this industry. His next move is into construction... and later, who knows! Every move shows Carl to be nimble-footed—to be able to shift gears in response to market needs, to move where the opportunity exists, and to create competencies as required, based on personal strengths to match market needs. The mark of an intuitive entrepreneur!

Case Study

Farhan worked for a ball bearing company in India for many years until he was bitten by the "entrepreneur bug". Encouraged by his ambitious and efficient wife, he quit his job and began importing and distributing ball bearings from the Eastern Europe. When this market became highly competitive and margins thinned, he moved to exporting clothing to the USA. This lasted while the going was good and when it turned bad, with competition from Thailand and China, Farhan moved to recruiting software personnel for US firms. Before the tide turned and software personnel began returning to India, Farhan had already read the writing on the wall. So he and his wife moved to the USA and did a "recon," what next?

They finally decided to venture into the real estate business, and they decided to move to an area in California, with a concentration of people of the Asian origin. He would then have a more receptive clientele, without color being a deterrent. Farhan worked as a subagent for an established estate agency. In the meantime, he took courses and examinations and was certified as an estate agent. Today, he runs his own agency. He advertises with large advertisements in the newspapers focused on US citizens of Indian origin. It is a target market. They have the money, and they have the need. It was again the right service to the right target customers at the right time. He did so well that now he lives in a luxurious home in California and drives a luxury car.

Case studies like those of Carl and Farhan are many.

Case Study

There is also the story of Evan Spiegel, the founder of messaging app Snapchat and the youngest billionaire in the world. Snapchat began life in a Stanford dorm room, but soon became the next big thing in the world of apps. The photo and video messaging app now gets nearly 4 billion video views every day.

Spiegel turned down an offer to sell his company for a reported $3 billion (₹19,000 crores). In 2015, just three years later, Snapchat is estimated to be valued at $16 billion. Forbes magazine now estimates Spiegel's net worth at $2.1 billion, even more than what has been quoted ($1.5 billion) earlier in this book.

ABILITY TO GRAB OPPORTUNITIES

Reading Ries and Trout's *Horse Sense* made me think of all the boys in school who had consistently stood first in class, year after year. I have not heard of most of them for a long, long time. Some joined the IFS and are yet to become ambassadors. Some joined the private sector and are yet to become CEOs. By the age of fifty-five, they should have. Some became doctors and lawyers and I know that they could do with some more "practice" or "clientele" just to make ends meet.

What put me into this reverie was Ries's statement that "in the dairy, cream rises to the top." In daily life, it's generally not true. It's mostly milk at the top of the corporate bottle. "Intelligence is a two-edged sword." Too little and you can't cope with the corporate paperwork—writing memos, travel arrangements. Too much and you are out of touch with the reality. You suffer from the absentminded Professor Syndrome.

"Top executives come from the middle of the IQ curve." As the Harvard college president said to the faculty at the commencement of the term, "Be nice to your A students because they will come back and be your colleagues, but be exceptionally nice to your B and C students because they will come back and give us a new auditorium and a new science building."

Peter McColough, former Chairman of Xerox, made the same point about his Harvard School class of 1949. "The record of accomplishment corresponds negatively with the standing of the class." The top people did not do that well. The one-third in the middle did. The guys who got the highest marks tended to be in the middle in accomplishment.

Why is this? Why does success in the classroom generally not correlate with success in a profession? The smarter people are, the more they depend on themselves. After all, they know everything. They depend only on themselves to get ahead. Less intelligent people are more likely to look for others to help them up the ladder and to look for opportunities and grab them. I never wrote articles earlier. All I wrote as a working executive was memos, minutes and reports. Then, Bina, a student at a management college where I taught Marketing married a journalist, Dilip Thakore, Editor of the *Business World*. She spoke to her husband about me, because he was desperately looking around for someone to write a regular column on Marketing for the *Business World*. He asked me. I said I would try. That was thirty years ago. I have been writing two columns every month, ever since, and some more. I grabbed the opportunity, and not just said "No. I've never done it before." I, thus, became a "business journalist."

I had never lectured at an American business school before. But, on a visit to the USA in 1989 during a holiday, I used an introduction from Professor C. Northcote Parkinson (Parkinson's Law), with whom I had collaborated to write a book on marketing, to meet Professor Philip Kotler at the Kellogg Business School. Kotler was kind and gracious and invited me for lunch at the college. We had a long chat from noon to 2 PM, when he said that we will have to move because he had a class at 2.15 PM. I was beginning to say goodbye and thank you when he suggested that I take the class and talk to them about marketing in Asia. With some hesitation, I said YES. My talk was well received, although I had not prepared for it. That was the beginning of my annual visits to Kellogg to give some talks as a visiting professor for over twenty years. And then I extended it to other business schools like Drexel, URI, Cornell, Rady, and some others.

Opportunities do not just arise in the environment. They are not presented to us by others, as the earlier incidents show. They can be inherent in us. They can be accidents that we may take to be calamities but that we can turn them into opportunities.

A young singer with a fine soprano was assigned to perform *The End of a Perfect Day* for admiring relatives. When his adolescent voice cracked and broke at the family gathering, he discovered he had the ability to make people laugh. The singer-cum-comedian was Bob Hope.

The goal-oriented person would have said, "I am not going to let this incident stop me from becoming a professional singer." The hard work-oriented person would have said, "I have to practice more." *But successful people take advantage of accidents. They see an opportunity in a calamity and grab it.*

A PASSION FOR EXCELLENCE

There is a story told of a platoon of soldiers who were on a forced march. There was a great resentment. It showed on their faces. It showed in their stride. They seemed to drag themselves forward because they did not want to march. They had to because they were ordered to.

Yet, after the march was over, and the soldiers were now tired, but free, they had the option of going on a mountain hike or resting in their camps. Most went for hiking, felt exhilarated by the challenge posed by the mountain and returned late at night, tired but happy and smiling.

It is all about Passion. There are some who find "passion in their occupation." They are truly blessed because if they have the passion for their occupation, they will most likely also have a passion for excellence.

Take the case of R.K. Laxman (hereafter, R.K.), among the best political cartoonists in the world. He was passionate about political cartoons. One cannot imagine R.K. doing anything else. I once attended a demonstration conducted by R.K. at a Rotary meeting and it was a pleasure to see him. So facile, so fast, so entertaining, and so passionate! No wonder he was among the best in the whole world, and he kept at it until his eighties. Neither the *Times of India* nor R.K. could unloosen the chord that tied them to the "common man" (his cartoon character).

Some "find passion for a hobby outside their job." This is not so good but better than nothing. Commander Eric Lopez worked with me in a pharma company as a Distribution Manager. He had retired early from the Navy. He always did an adequate job, sometimes a good job. He was honest, sincere and hard working. But every evening he waited for the clock to strike 5.30 so he could be off to his home and his passion, playing the wooden saw with a violin bow. He was perhaps the only one who did this. And he was invited to give performances in different parts of India and even abroad, in Israel and Russia. He taught his two daughters this unusual technique and sometimes one of them accompanied him. It was a heart-warming "sight" and soothing music to our "ears". Lopez spent most of his nonworking hours practicing on the musical saw. It was his passion. A passion he found in his hobby rather than in his work.

And there are those who find a passion in what they do, only after the end of their working life—in their retirement—like my friend Felix Fernandez down the road who retired from BPL, a petroleum company, after thirty-two years, and then began growing roses. He got so good at this, that he was elected President of The Rose Society of Mumbai. He developed some unusual rose grafts. He grew more roses of different varieties. Many five star hotels became his clients. Ferntastica Gardens evolved from a passion to a big business. "Too little, too late," will you say? Well, with passion, "better late than never."

HOW YOU MAKE YOUR OWN DESTINY

I was presented with a book called *Pathbreakers 2*, which is published by Kensource Business Books, featuring twenty-five outstanding people in India who have "excelled" in whatever they did and made India proud. I wish a publication like this was available more easily to the young people on the threshold of their careers. I feel that ₹1,300 for a well-produced book is a lot of money; although, for a coffee table, it is a good "value for money" book. Perhaps, libraries could buy a copy and then people can read this tome without the large money outlay.

Why am I talking about *Pathbreakers*? Because among the twenty-five, which includes persons like Amitabh Bachchan (film idol) and Hemendra Kothari (stock broker), there is a large number of people who have fought the odds of very humble beginnings to reach the top of the profession. They are the ones who had the grit, the determination, the perseverance, the courage, the patience and the ability to keep learning, to take risks and to finally reach the pinnacle of success. For me, it is another eye opener that in a country where "money talks", where influence is of great importance, where the law acts lightly on those with money and influence, there are people who can still beat the system and come out on top. It shows us that the American concept of meritocracy still works in scattered islands in the country. There are many who crook a finger at the system and say "I will be there at the peak, in spite of you." And this is a message of hope for all those below twenty-five. There is a whole new world of opportunities in India waiting for you, if you have a goal, the passion, and determination to get to the peak.

One of those featured in *Pathbreakers 2* is Dr Ram Buxani, who came to India penniless after the Partition, had lost his father as a child and started his career as a typist in Mumbai. He left Indian shores in 1959 for Dubai when there was no power, water or airport. Dr Buxani was just a good typist without a college degree in search of a better life. But he went on to become a successful businessman in Dubai, a multimillionaire and the voice of the nonresident Indian, especially, the Sindhi community. He completed his Ph.D. a few years ago with a dissertation on the tribal tradition in decision-making in Dubai.

There is Shamrao Chougule, who used to cut grass and look after cattle in a village near Kolhapur, as a child. Yet, this man was able to produce India's first champagne quality wine. Chougule is a story of passion and determination. He moved from selling tubular structures to setting up a fabrication business, which took him to the Gulf, and then to France, where he fell in love with champagne. The rest is history. Shamrao Chougule, virtually singlehandedly created a wine culture in India. He waited for seventeen years to make money.

Dr Anil Khandelwal had a tough childhood of hardship and discrimination. He went to a Hindi medium municipal school. The joint family had disowned his father. He wore altered hand me downs from his cousins. He did not know any English till sixth standard. And yet, with passion and determination, he became the chairman of the Bank of Baroda. No other bank chairman in the country is as academically qualified as Khandelwal; he is B.Sc., BE, MBA, LLB, Ph.D. with post graduate diplomas in Labour Law and Training and Development. Under his chairmanship (this poor boy from Agra), Bank of Baroda moved up a solid 158 places in the ranking of top 1,000 banks in the world from 416 in 2006 to 258 in 2007.

And there are others who teach those of us who want to listen: "What man has done, man can do." You can too!

CHANGING TRACKS TO DIFFERENT STATIONS

I have written earlier that in the twenty-first century, young people will not look for a long-term career with companies. They will look for assignments: short-term, mostly; medium-term, many times; long-term, sometimes. There is now a completely different attitude toward the concept of loyalty. But we will deal with this in depth at another time.

We have also talked about how young people change jobs from banking to catering and from oil company executives to floriculture.

We now need to see how it is possible to keep diverting from one's original goal to something else, quite unexpected, quite different and yet, quite successful.

Gautam Rajadhyaksha is now a famous photographer. He is one of the pioneers in Bollywood. His photo portraits of some of the superstars of Bollywood, of yesteryear and the present, have been widely acclaimed. Gautam went to St Xavier's College, Mumbai and did a Bachelor's in Science, majoring in Microbiology. Is there anything in common between peering through the lens of a microscope and peering through the lens of a camera? One does not know. You will have to ask Gautam.

Much before him, another luminary studied Microbiology and did a Bachelor's in Science. It was Gerson da Cunha, who took the degree and went on to take a job in journalism with *Times of India*. Then he went into copy-writing with an advertising agency, finally to head the agency—Lintas. Then he went to UNICEF to administer their programs in Brazil, and then to India in retirement, to organize and head AGNI—the nongovernment organization which fights to ensure good governance by our municipal corporation and our state government. Surely, it was a long way from B.Sc. (Microbiology) to Chief Coordinator of AGNI.

I met Sukdev at the University of Rhode Island (URI) Business School in the USA in April 2007. He was coordinating a program on International Marketing and Entrepreneurship. I asked him what he was doing earlier. He said that he was in the IAS and after seven years in the service, he decided to quit and pursue Ph.D. and teach undergrads. His basic academic background had not prepared him for such assignments, yet he did well. He was very popular with the students, whom he continuously challenged to think wider and deeper to come to conclusions which were off the beaten track.

Shoba De was a fashion model who went into journalism, became editor of Stardust, the Bollywood gossip magazine, and then went on to becoming a good-selling author, who now teaches creative writing at foreign universities. And she neither had a qualification in journalism nor in creative writing.

Few people know that Jawaharlal Nehru did a Bachelor's in Botany when in college in the UK. And from Botany, he went into politics to finally leave an indelible imprint on India.

So do not worry about your basic degree. It is an "entry" ticket. You may use it temporarily for a few years and then move on. Or you may see an alignment and stay on and like Gerson's colleague, Yvonne Freitas, go on doing Ph.D. in Microbiology and be appointed the head of the department of Microbiology at St Xavier's College, Mumbai, many years later.

There are people, like Gautam and Gerson, who use their academic qualifications as an entry point and then move on to different things. There are those who use the qualification to build on it and stay with the specialty with single-minded determination. Both succeed. What will you do?

Flexibility in a career is about nimble footedness, about courage, about a positive outlook, and a spirit of "never say die."

CAREER FLEXIBILITY AND DIGNITY OF LABOR

My son, who lives in California, has a housekeeper, a Mexican woman who comes twice a week and gives the house a thorough "spruce up". She does such an excellent job that even my four-year-old granddaughter, on returning from school, joyously exclaims, "Oh Carmen was here!" Carmen's husband worked for an IT company in town. With the meltdown, he lost his job. Now John accompanies Carmen on her rounds and they do the jobs together. As a result, they complete each home now in half the time. And they have begun accepting more assignments since they have more time. Did John feel bad about making the change from an IT office to working as a housekeeper? Did he feel ashamed? Did he resent working with his wife? He felt none of these things.

John was happy doing what he needed to do and earning a living "by the sweat of his brow" rather than sitting and mopping about his glorious past and the bleak future. And he hopes that he will get back to his IT job when things improve, either in the same company or some other.

John showed me how one can change gears and face life stoically in adversity.

On another occasion, I began talking to Tony, the mason who was doing work in the same house in California. I asked him how long he has been doing masonry work and I was surprised to know it was only three years. "Really? And what did you do before that?" I asked him. He told me he was a commercial airline pilot for fifteen years, had worked for American Airlines, and was laid off when the company began flying downhill. With the whole airline industry being in trouble, he did not want to just wait on the sidelines. It is also expensive to keep the flying license alive. So what did he do?

He had always liked masonry work. He decided to attend some courses and qualify as a certified mason. Now he is enjoying this career and earning good money in the process. Perhaps, he is not earning as much as he would have earned as a commercial pilot but nothing to be sniffed at either. And then, who knows when the world economy improves again, perhaps, he would resume flying—which still is his first love.

Hai Wan is an expert on how to do business in China. She is now so well-known that she was asked to be the official interpreter when the Deputy Prime Minister of China visited the US. She has a Ph.D. in Sociology and has taught at the US universities. The second time we had a meal together, I found that she left an inordinately large tip. The tip in the US is more than in most countries. And she always left even more. I could not help mentioning this to Hai Wan that she was extraordinarily generous. She looked at me with a faraway look in her eyes. She said,

> You know Walter, when I first came to the US from China, I worked as a waitress. And I worked long hours to be

able to pay for board and lodge and finance my education. I was always happy when customers left generous tips for good service. I went out of my way to provide such service. I have not forgotten those days. Today, I am on the other side of the table. I am doing for them, what I expected to be done to me.

Hai Wan had changed careers. She had grown in knowledge, in stature, and in affordability. She grew into a future without forgetting the past. She took up a new and upscale profession from a more run-of-the mill job. Tony moved consciously and deliberately from a highflying job to a down to earth profession without remorse or regret. John took on what was conveniently available and made the best of it, waiting for the tide to come in again.

Lessons for all of us, in flexibility, in fortitude, and the dignity of labor!

3

Have a Vision
The Big Picture

> *Having a vision is extremely important. It is critical to decide where you want to be five or ten years hence, and then work backward, how you will get there. This may apply to an individual career or a company objective.*
>
> **Adi Godrej**
> Chairman, Godrej Industries Ltd.,
> Former President, Confederation of
> Indian Industry (CII)

There are only a few people having a clear vision of what they want to do in life, when they are very young. Most young boys will tell you that they want to become policemen, pilots, or cab drivers. These are just passing fads.

A certain vision gets defined as we grow older, and we have the capacity to understand our strengths and weaknesses. The person who has defined his vision has, perhaps, seen the invisible, felt the intangible, and then strives to achieve the impossible. As he moves forward, the vision becomes clearer, and what needs to be done becomes more defined.

Case Study

I had no aptitude for mathematics in school; therefore, I did biological sciences and chemistry in college and went on to specialize in pharmaceutical technology. I then joined a large multinational, Glaxo, as a management trainee, where I was guided into specializing in marketing. The Company felt I could optimize my strengths to combine technical knowledge with communication skills. After a successful corporate career, spanning 14 years, I transferred to being an entrepreneur as an early marketing consultant in the country. It has been a good run and I have completed forty years as a marketing consultant and trainer working across the globe.

Did I have this vision when I finished high school? Certainly not.

The Vision got defined as I moved further down the road and finally saw a light at the end of the tunnel.

UNUSUAL EXAMPLES

- I saw a TV show sometime back where a four-year-old played Western classical music on the piano with fine aplomb, without any notes. Truly, the boy is a genius! He will probably have his vision by six years of age, of what he will do and where he will go. He is different from most of us.
- The *Times of India* reported on July 25, 2015, that golf prodigy, Shubam Jagtar, the ten-year-old

son of a milkman in India, has scored another hit in the US. After the IMG Academy Junior World Championship win in San Diego, he has swung his way to the ITGA World Stars of Junior Golf Crown in Las Vegas.

All of us have to objectively and rationally assess what we will do and where we will go, so that the hard work which is always necessary to get to the goal of achievement, success, and contentment (ASC) is not wasted on a chimera.

YOUR CAPABILITY (WHAT CAN YOU DO?)

Case Study

I was an impatient manager in my time. In my first company, Glaxo, when I was special assistant to the sales director, after finishing the management training period, I initiated market research in the company in the early sixties to look at potential for products where Glaxo would have an advantage. Two years and six reports later—some of which were implemented—a senior manager was inducted from the failed consumer product division of another multinational company. The Board felt that the company should now have an expanded market research division, and I was considered too young to head it. After the senior manager joined—and I reported to him—I found he knew so little that I had to cover for him all the time. The products we were dealing with had a technical slant, and he faced difficulties as he was not qualified in pharma technology. I was virtually running a pharma class for him, and I was not learning anymore. In fact, I was teaching. I decided to move to another company where a "young age" is not a barrier for becoming a senior manager. I left Glaxo to join a fresh startup, a US-based multinational pharma company. The impatient manager in me had acted. I never regretted this move or the move made two years later—again, moving to a senior position. The pastures were greener on this side and there was no looking back.

YOUR CAPACITY (HOW MUCH CAN YOU DO?)

Case Study

The managing director of this American conglomerate had great dreams. He was impatient, not only for himself but also for the company. He wanted to run both fast and sure. His small, young, and effective team had delivered excellent results in the first two years since the start of the company, but he wanted to go faster. So he went shopping for high value senior managers from large companies who could deliver higher growth. He first brought in a "good personality" who talked more than he could deliver. It took just six months to assess John and know it was a mistake. So his area of operation was reduced from both divisions of the company to only one; however, his designation of marketing director was retained. The CEO then brought in a senior advertising executive as the marketing director of the consumer product division. It turned out to be another failure, and it took just four months to discover that. This mistake was sought to be corrected by bringing in an overall chief marketing director from among the largest multinational consumer product companies. It was not for nothing that this new chief had not been promoted for eight years in his previous company. So, this correction also ended up in creating yet another problem.

Many lessons were learnt: the CEO made mistakes in assessing capabilities and the capacity of his existing managers and of each new manager. The new managers themselves had made mistakes in assessing their own capabilities in their anxiety to move up the ladder. Everyone lost, except members of the original team who left one after the other to new assignments in other companies—to greener pastures which existed and which they had not known.

Thanks to an impatient boss, they looked for and found other doors opening to them, and built careers which they would otherwise have missed.

Have a Vision: The Big Picture

The leader should have the ability to transform vision into reality. The real vision requires an ability to understand consumer's behavior, competitive dynamics, and deep commitment to build competency. Above all, it requires an ability to be comfortable with ambiguity and uncertainty.

> *The leader requires a number of personal qualities. He should be able to share a vision with simplicity, lucidity, and clarity with his team. It is a team effort and goal. He should be inspiring, fair, and transparent. He should be able to earn the trust of all his stake holders—customers, employees, shareholders, vendors, and the financial community. A leader is actually a risk taker and works for long-term and not just for short-term success or goals.*
>
> *The business cannot survive for a long-term, if it is aligned only to animal instinct of profits and not to community interest. Therefore, true visionary leaders are required to create sustained and continuous value for the community in which they operate. They are not followers. They create their own path of success.*
>
> **Habil Khorakiwala**
Chairman, Wockhardt Ltd., India

MISDIRECTED LIFE GOALS

I was once asked to address a training program for new recruits in the Indian Accounts and Audit Service (IAAS) at their college in Nagpur. When I was there, I was surprised to know that over fifty percent of the trainees were from UP, Bihar, and Orissa. Just these three states! There were none from Gujarat and Punjab, and just a few from some of the other states.

I was wondering about such disproportionate representation at a national institute for an all-India cadre. Later, I was provided with a rational explanation by one of the participants. He said that there were fewer industries in that part of the country; therefore, lesser job opportunities. A job in the Central Government cadre is an even more prestigious assignment. And an appointment through a competitive examination was a highpoint in the achievement.

Thus, those who got selected to the IAS, IPS, and IAAS, in that order, commanded the highest dowries. Those whose assignments would enable them to have alternate sources of income would get even bigger dowries than those who would not have such opportunities. The IAAS (with IRS) was, therefore, a favored institution and candidates who got selected had their life plan of success laid out before them. It was a revelation to me. Also, something that shocked and surprised me.

Are there people who set goals of accumulating "black" money and work out a whole life plan to enable them to do this? Is it something openly and brazenly accepted by society, even though it may be left unsaid and not openly discussed? Can these goals, when choosing a career, be something that you would choose to do through your whole working life? Having opportunities galore or creating them, do you extort money from the "money bags," as you perceive them, who have paid for their earnings in sweat, sometimes tears and even blood?

The setting of life goals has to have a "noble aim." It has to provide intellectual, emotional, and spiritual satisfaction. For different people, methods may be different, based on their nature and nurture and on their ability and capability. But the direction has to remain the same. The arrow has to point in the same direction though the arching of the bow may differ.

To begin life with even the vague notion of earning a lot or even some "black" money is a repulsive thought and an audacious concept. Surely black money can be earned in most spheres of life—in business, in government service, in the professions as doctors, lawyers, engineers, surveyors, and so on. But it cannot be the prime objective in choosing a career.

If one does this, one will only regret it at the end of a career to look back at a wasted life where one looked for the pot of gold for life's total fulfillment and could not find it. It is then too late to retract.

WHAT CAN YOU CONTRIBUTE?

At a certain time of the year, there is much talk about campus recruitment, especially at the major management colleges. They talk about priority companies and priority industries, which one will get the first opportunity to hire the brightest and the best. A new format has been suggested for this year by one of the IIMs—where they will have all from one industry available at one time, to make it easier for both recruiters and candidates. And as always, there is a lot of talk about the highest salary offered this year, which was lower than the highest salary offered last year. Obviously, it was a spin off from the effect of the two-year recession, especially on the financial sector. Students are rated on the basis of salary offered. And, even the institutions are rated based on the average salary offered to their students.

I wonder whether there is any emphasis on "contribution." What will the young person expect to contribute, for his salary, to the company and its clients and to the community that it serves? Does the question of "contribution" ever cross the mind of the young person? And, if it does not, is it that we have somehow failed in instilling this value during the school and college career? Who are the role models in India, successful in their career and also great contributors to the community and the country? I would focus on just three of them who have influenced this vast country of 1.2 billion people. There are many, many others, who have had regional impact, which is also a great contribution.

One such significant contributor is Dr Varghese Kurian, the founder of the Kaira District Milk Cooperative Society in Gujarat. Almost single-handedly, this dairy technologist from Kerala went into the alien soil in Gujarat and within a few decades became the author of the "white revolution." India, which was importing milk powder earlier and was a milk deficit country, has converted into a milk surplus country. Amul became a household name. Amul had milk to spare to enable it to venture into branded butter, cheese, curd, and chocolate. Dr V. Kurian not only had a successful career, but he also helped to change the country. He will always be remembered.

Another significant contributor was Dr M.S. Swaminathan, the eminent agricultural scientist. Yes, he pursued a career in agriculture but went beyond that sphere of life. He created the green revolution in India, the same way as Kurian created the white revolution. New methods of cultivation were taken to remote areas of the country to make sure that yields were now multifold than what they were earlier. India no longer needed to import grain. In fact, India could export food grains. Thanks to the contribution of Dr M.S. Swaminathan! He helped to change the country. He will always be remembered.

Yet another significant contributor, but not so well known, is Bindeshwar Pathak, the engineer from the Public Works Department of the Bihar Government, who developed a new sewage system which used very little water and where the sewage could be used to generate gas. He did not get much support for his innovative development, so he quit the service and, with encouragement and loans from friends, started Sulabh International

Social Service Organization. In a short time, Sulabh toilets spread around the country. It provided an alternative to the physical carrying of night soil.

People engaged in this activity earlier were provided with more dignified jobs as monitors at Sulabh toilets. Earlier, bathing and use of toilets were free for women and children, whereas men were charged a small fee. Toilets are kept clean by the monitors. In spite of the free admissions, Sulabh toilets still made a profit. The gas from Sulabh toilets in Patna helps to provide electricity to the Patna General Hospital.

There is no sanitation system in much of India. Over fifty percent of the population in cities, like Mumbai, lives in slums, on pavements, and have no regular toilet facilities. Pathak saw this crying need. He also saw that the Government and Municipalities were not providing a solution. So he developed a unique solution. So unique that he is now a UN expert taken around the world for advising authorities in Africa and South America.

One day he will be recognized as a significant contributor to the community in India. Someone who took up a problem, everyone else shied from, and found an effective and economical solution.

Kurian, Swaminathan, and Pathak had careers. They worked for money. But they looked beyond to see how they could make a contribution. It was not just the "highest salary." It was the balance of money—what do I get—and contribution—what do I give.

THE GLORY IS IN THE STRIVING

When you study Maslow's hierarchy of human needs, you realize that the final striving of all of us is for "self-actualization." Food, clothing, shelter, and sex are all needs way below in the hierarchy. It is the self-esteem and self-actualization that people finally search for and work for.

I spent time doing some work for the Aditya Birla Group many years ago and had some interaction with that legend of the Indian industry, Aditya Birla. One day when he was discussing a new multimillion-dollar project, which was also the first in the country and a risky one, I asked him why he was going into this. "Don't you already have more than twenty companies in the group and enough problems to keep your hands full?" I asked. He looked at me for some time with a faraway look in his eyes. "Mr Vieira," he said,

> When God has given me so much, I need to make use of the wealth to generate more wealth. Not just wealth for me. I cannot eat or drink anymore or dress any better or holiday more. I need to keep expanding to provide more jobs to new people, to provide more opportunities to existing people, to use the natural resources of our country, and to make this a better world. Personally, one more project will make little difference to my personal wealth and to my present standard of living. But it will make a big difference to thousands of other people who perhaps have no job at present.

This industrialist, Aditya Birla, was on a journey of self-actualization. Sure, he wanted to be recognized, to be among the biggest industrialists in India, to grow in self-esteem, to be proud of his achievements, and to be a path breaker.

At a certain point, you move away from just cash and yourself to the achievement and others, the community. You do not just hang up your boots and say "enough is enough." It may be enough for you. But there is far more to be done to be enough for all the others who are less fortunate.

I, therefore, understood the talk that was given by Warren Buffet at Washington University, Seattle, at their convocation some years ago. Warren Buffet is the second richest man in the world after Bill Gates. He is the founder of Berkshire Investments and has a large following worldwide. After his speech, he was asked by some of the students, "Mr Buffet, what will you do with the $60 billion that you have? Will you leave it for your children?" And Warren Buffet replied, "No, I will leave much of it for charities to improve the world. I will leave just enough for my children so that they are not in need. But not so much that they do not have to work." What an interesting answer!

Warren Buffet lives in an old home which is not luxurious, drives a "not posh" car, and lives a simple life. But he keeps making more money for Berkshire and its shareholders with his genius for investments. Why does he do it? Self-satisfaction, not just "more cash."

4

Be Innovative, Be Different
Understand Consumer Needs

"Be daring, be different, be impractical, be anything that will assert integrity of purpose and imaginative vision against the play-it-safers, the creatures of the commonplace, the slaves of the ordinary."
—**Sir Cecil Beaton** (1904–1980),
Photographer and designer

Hard work has to be relevant. Those who spend the whole month digging holes and then filling them up also put in hard work. But, it is a useless pursuit.

Those who make a mark are innovative. They want to be different, not just for the sake of being different but for the sake of making a difference to the final consumer/user. They keep meeting new consumer needs or old needs with faster, better, and cheaper solutions with fewer hassles. These are the impatient managers who succeed.

> Innovation is the specific instrument of entrepreneurship. The act that endows resources with a new capacity to create wealth.
>
> *Peter Drucker*
> *Management Consultant*

Be Innovative, Be Different: Understand Consumer Needs

I believe Innovation, is not just about doing different things but also doing things differently. As a first generation entrepreneur, I have learnt that innovation creates value and differentiation builds competitive advantage. When I started Biocon, I was driven by the spirit to create a business that would leverage science for the benefit of society through affordable innovation. That has always been Biocon's raison d'être.

In India, Biocon pioneered the development of biotech drugs, which are difficult-to-make, complex, and expensive therapies to fight chronic, life-threatening conditions. However, we chose to do this through disruptively innovative process engineering that could deliver affordable pricing. As a patient-centric organization, we addressed the relatively unmet needs of patients by bringing advanced biopharmaceuticals against diabetes and cancer at price points that made them affordable and, thus, accessible. Biocon has, thus, made a significant impact on global health by rationalizing healthcare spends and enhancing access to affordable biotherapeutics.

In today's world, technology is playing a transformational role in enabling innovation and driving change. I believe the entrepreneurial energy of today's youth can leverage the power of innovation to deliver superior and sustainable solutions for a better life and a brighter future. However, for an innovative idea to become a successful enterprise it must address the unmet needs of its customers, only then a meaningful value creation will take place. If I could

> *build a billion dollar business on the foundation of innovative ideas and meager resources, with no business experience but the abundant spirit and youthful confidence, I believe anyone can do so.*
>
> **Kiran Mazumdar Shaw**
> Chairman and Managing Director
> Biocon Ltd., India

THINK DIFFERENTLY, BE DIFFERENT!

Whatever you do, wherever you go, you will be a winner if you think differently and be different. You can start being different when you are in high school, when you're in college, or when you have begun a working career. Some of us are born with a "questioning mind" and may end up with an attitude of destructive disobedience to the great dismay of our parents, teachers, and bosses. Others among us are also born with a questioning mind but with an attitude of "constructive disobedience." They are found welcomed in the corporate world and are often encouraged by progressive organizations to become "intrapreneurs," that is, act as independent entrepreneurs (or businessmen) but work within the boundaries of the organization.

There is no limit to how and when one can think differently. I was once stuck on a highway because I ran out of fuel. The fuel gauge was not working. Fortunately, I was only three km away from a petrol station and I had an empty plastic can in the boot which could be used to bring enough fuel to start the car. The petrol stations were forbidden from selling or lending cans—the government's attempt to curb the sales of "loose fuel." My son Samir, then ten, was with me and we managed to get a cab to the petrol station, bought four liters of fuel, paid the attendant, and then found the can was leaking. There was a crack at the base of the can. Will the attendant help and loan us a can just for fifteen minutes till we bring the car? No way. All our pleading fell on deaf ears. Samir suggested, "But dad why don't we just seal the mouth of the can and turn it upside down." It was an obvious solution which had not struck the pump attendant or me. That's what we did. We went back to the car and solved our problem. Samir thought differently; he looked for a solution rather than just moaning about a problem. In retrospect, it seemed so obvious and so simple. Always in retrospect! Samir is now an entrepreneur, running an event management company, and still thinking on his feet.

When you look around, there are so many things that could be different, better, perhaps cheaper. I read in the *Times of India* some weeks ago about a US scientist who had used corn residues to develop a novel packaging film that could destroy Listeria monocytogene, a rod-shaped bacterium that causes food poisoning in animals and humans. It is a biodegradable polylactic acid (PLA) film, from a renewable material. What a fantastic idea! Why did not anyone think of this before? It is because Tony Jin of the US Department of Agriculture in Pennsylvania thought differently and, thus, made a difference to the US and to the world.

And of course, there is a time and place for all new ideas. Many ideas are before their time and, therefore, do no create an impact. These new ideas must find fertile ground so that the seeds will germinate and sprout and grow into plants. Would Amazon.com, eBay, Naukri.com, or Shaadi.com have been a success fifteen or even ten years ago? Who knows, but it is unlikely. It needed a certain population of computers and a certain population with a receptive mindset to enable them to be a big success. These were great ideas delivered to us in palatable packaging just as we are hungry for them.

However, this may be a "tipping point" when it pays to think differently and be different. Even if eight out of ten seeds fall on the arable land and only two fall on the fertile ground and these ideas succeed, it can change either the immediate environment, the community, country, and sometimes, the world.

DIFFERENTIATE, SEGMENT, FOCUS

In the study of marketing, there are three concepts that are critical in the success of products and services. First, "differentiate" your offering so it is different from all others in the market place. It is not an imitation. You are not an "also ran." Second, "segment" your market because you cannot offer one product to all customers. The prospective customers for an expensive Rolex are different from the customers for an inexpensive Citizen or HMT watch. Third, you "position" the product in the customers mind—a five star Taj Hotel at the Gateway of India compared to a one star Residency hotel in a distant suburb of Santa Cruz. Marketers will keep repeating the mantra of "differentiate, differentiate, differentiate!"

Many years ago there was an article published with the title "Why can't you sell brotherhood like soap?" It propagated the thesis that even causes like "Cancer Aid" or "World Wildlife Fund for Nature" can be, and should be, sold like soap using similar approaches and thinking. The more one thinks about it, the more one gets convinced. Why not?

Why can we not sell ourselves like products, become a brand, differentiate, segment, and position, especially at a time and in an environment where all three are possible and it is not like the "not so good old days"?

When Dr Punshi, came back from the USA fifty years ago with a Ph.D. in petroleum technology, he could not get a suitable job to fit in with his specialization. The petrochemical industry in India was in its infancy. Since opportunities were limited, he joined Glaxo, a pharmaceutical company in the early 1950s and finally rose to be a senior covenanted manager in pharmaceutical production. He did well by the social standards, but he had differentiated in an area where the segment did not exist. And, he had to take a diversion!

Now forty years later, my friend Shanker's son specialized in wildlife conservation. He pioneered the first turtle farm in the country on the beaches of Chennai, built a reputation in wildlife conservation, and now runs a successful outfit in this field with headquarters in Bangalore. He does excellent work, gets funding from international agencies and government, and what is more important, he is enjoying himself doing what he always wanted to do. He is proving the truth of the old adage that "when your work is also your hobby, you will not have to work a single day of your life."

When my friend Hari Menon told me twenty years ago that his son has joined the Zee Institute for Multimedia to specialize in animation technology, I must say I was slightly skeptical. "Is there scope for work in this area?" I asked. He said that his son thinks there is. And in any case, he is besotted with Walt Disney cartoons and the whole world of animation. Today, young Menon is one of the stars in the animation field, much sought after by firms that are producing animation films for India and producing films for foreign companies who find that they can get good work from India at lower costs. When Menon's friends graduated in English literature, physics, or chemistry, Menon took the less beaten path. He differentiated his training, segmented potential employers, and positioned himself as an expert in a lesser-known field where he came to be a pioneer.

Again, we go back to the basic rules in identifying talent and choosing careers. What can you do? What are your capabilities and natural talents? What would you like to do? What are you passionate about?

By matching the two, of what you can do and what you would like to do, you are able to fit the "glove to the hand"—an ideal situation which often does not happen!

Imagination is everything. It is the preview of life's coming attractions.

Albert Einstein,
Physicist

Innovation has nothing to do with how many R&D dollars you have. It's not about money. It's about the people you have, how you're led, and how much you get it.

Steve Jobs,
CEO of Apple

Think big, think fast, think ahead. Ideas are no one's monopoly.

Dhirubhai Ambani,
Founder, Reliance Industries

HOW DOES ONE BECOME A SUCCESSFUL ENTREPRENEUR?

Narayan Murthy, cofounder and former chairman of Infosys and one of the most successful entrepreneurs in India, had this to say in the *Times of India* of August 21, 2015, on "How does one become a successful entrepreneur?"

> Entrepreneurship is about converting the power of an idea into jobs, into wealth for oneself, into wealth for others, and prosperity for the country.
>
> Therefore, an entrepreneur must be able to express his or her idea in a simple sentence.
>
> Second, that sentence must convey the differentiated value proposition of that idea that means how that idea is better than all the existing products and services.
>
> Third, an entrepreneur must validate the thought of that idea by some kind of test marketing. Otherwise he or she will spend a lot of time and money and will realize that this idea is not going to work.
>
> Fourth, an entrepreneur must bring together a team that has a complimentary skill set, for instance, some people should know technology, some people should know finance, some should know sales and marketing, and some should know HR etcetera.

Narayan Murthy did all the above and created one of the most successful companies in India within two decades and became an "Icon."

In the last few decades, there have been so many innovators who conveyed "the differentiated value proposition" to the consumer then tested the proposition, found acceptance, and then built multimillion dollar empires with, sometimes, very simple innovations.

Case Study

In the 1960s when I worked for Glaxo, I used to visit many small towns and villages in India. I sometimes used to see long queues of men at chemist shops and initially I wondered what they were patiently waiting to buy. Then I found out that they were waiting in the queue to buy hair oil by the "cap full" for a few coins. They had it poured onto their palm, rubbed it across both palms, and then gave their head a good massage. I was told that they could not afford to buy a full bottle of hair oil at one time. So they bought a cap full, whenever they could afford it.

Did I do anything with this information? Nothing! Nor did anyone else from the thousands who witnessed this phenomenon do anything.

It was in the 1980s that Mr C.K. Ranganathan from Chennai met this need and put hair oil and hair shampoo in plastic sachets and sold it under the brand name Velvette at the price of a "cap full." Not only did poor people buy this product but also many of the rich bought sachets for convenience in travel and for handy use. In just a few years, CavinKare evolved into a multimillion company. The giants in this field, like Levers and P&G, began to feel the heat of the competition. This showed in the growth of sales or the lack of it. It forced them to introduce their brands in smaller packages. CavinKare had shown the way with a simple innovation, in packaging.

Case Study

Another innovator noticed that most of the washing of clothes was done manually by poor people in India. Even in affluent households, the washing was done by house help. They did not really want or need a fancy soap with fancy perfume. A simple functional cheap bar of soap is all that is required. Thus, Nirma washing soap was born from the innovative mind of Karsanbhai Patel in Ahmedabad. The product was introduced, supported by heavy advertising and wide distribution, and ensured by large discounts to retailers. They recommended Nirma to new users and convinced existing users of other brands of washing soap to switch. Nirma was such an astounding success that Levers had to reinvent itself and introduce another product in the same price segment, Wheel. In the meantime, Nirma became a multimillion company.

Case Study

At a time when world oil prices went up, and consequently, the prices of glass bottles as well as transportation kept going north, a young man in Ahmedabad, India, Piruz Khambatta introduced a "powder juice" in cartons. A spoonful of powder could be added to a glass of water with some sugar to taste and you would have a glass of orange squash at home. It is much cheaper because of the low transport cost (no liquid bulk), no breakages (no glass bottles), and no sugar content. Rasna soon became a household name and Khambatta became a millionaire.

Rasna left all the reputed squash and juice manufacturers far behind in the race toward the consumers' wallet.

Case Study

It is the same with the world of e-commerce now. Many people say that Flipkart is a "copy" of the Amazon.com model. In a certain manner, it is a copy of the Amazon model; in others, it is not since it changed the entire delivery system. Indians are not used to making online payments, so Flipkart introduced cash on delivery (CoD). With this arrangement, the total profile of online purchase changed and Flipkart became a success story in terms of revenue and valuation. After raising $1 billion, Sachin and Binny Bansal have set their sights on making Flipkart a $100 billion entity by valuation in the next few years from $7 billion now in 2015. They wish to be the first $100 billion internet company from India with an enlarged focus on e-commerce and logistics.

Although Amazon trailed Flipkart for some time, it has now also adopted the CoD model, so that they can continue in the game and has now once again overtaken Flipkart in this very interesting race.

There are many others in the e-commerce space—Myntra, Snapdeal, Taxi for Sure, Job.com, Housing.com—and thousands of others coming on board every year. Each one of them tries to meet a need, such as

- Sidhant Pai of Photoprint Solutions aims to standardize the size and quality of 3D printer filaments by transforming plastic waste into raw material for 3D printers. It obtains the raw material for 3D printers using low cost machines and employing local waste pickers.
- Anirudh Sharma has developed a "Haptic Shoe for visually impaired" which can help the visually impaired people to find their way with four vibration actuators on each side of the shoe and interactions happening via a smart phone into which they can voice input their destination.
- Hemant Satyanarayana has developed TrialAR or a Trial room using Augmented Reality—a technology that lets you try clothes digitally without having to wear them.
- Dr Shyam V. Rao developed 3 Nethra, which combines four screening devices into a portable battery powered device, which anybody can be trained to operate. It takes the image of the eye, analyzes it, and comes up with a diagnosis on its own. The testing procedure takes just five minutes and can detect five eye ailments which contribute to ninety percent of avoidable blindness in India.
- Mansukhbhai Prajapati developed the clay pot Mitticooler refrigerator, which is cost effective and does not need electricity. He followed it up with developing a nonstick clay pan and later with a clay

cooker and a thermos made of clay. Forbes magazine named him as "India's most powerful rural entrepreneur" and National Geographic has named him the "Nat GeoEco Hero."
- Prateek Bumb and Aniruddha Sharma have developed a process for removing carbon dioxide from gaseous effluents to the extent of ninety percent and recovering the CO_2 to be sold as a product to other users later, for example, manufacturers of industrial gases and carbonated drinks.

There are many others mentioned in the book *Indian Innovators* by Akshat Agrawal.[1]

They are all trying to find a niche of unmet needs and if the numbers are large enough, they succeed. If they have overestimated the need or the product is not properly tailored, they fail. This is where innovation has to be combined with marketing and both must march hand in hand. Unfortunately, this does not always happen.

Each Innovator has to answer the three questions posed by Arthur Felton many years ago:

- Is there a need, but no market?
- Is there a market, but no customer?
- Is there a customer, but no salesman to inform him?

From the answers to these questions, the marketing strategy will follow:

- What to make?
- Whom to offer?
- How to deliver?

---
[1] Akshat Agrawal, *Indian Innovators* (Jaico, 2015).

For the innovator, as for the rest of us, the goal remains the same, embodied in the crisp definition, proffered by Philip Kotler, the guru of marketing: "To provide customer satisfaction, at a profit to yourself, making optimum use of available resources."

It was for a reason that the late Peter Drucker, the high priest of management, repeatedly said, "There are only 2 revenue centres in the company: innovation and marketing. All the rest are costs."

Therefore, innovators must ensure that their innovation fits into a real need, where the customer will find value in paying the price. Some of the questions posed by marketers, whether brick and mortar (b/m) or e-commerce, are:[2]

1. How can we spot and choose the right market segment/s to serve?
A company failed in aggregation of superior hotel rooms but succeeded with lower priced hotel room aggregation—OYO rooms.
2. How can we differentiate our offering from competitive offerings?
Flipkart came much after Amazon, but offered the customer cash on delivery instead of payment only by card on the net-banking. It quickly stole a march and beat Amazon in the marketplace.
3. How should we respond to customers who press us for a lower price?
E-commerce now offers a wide range of prices, so wide that the customer is spoiled for choices.
4. How can we compete against lower cost, lower price competitors from here and abroad?

---

[2] These questions are taken from Philip Kotler's book, *Marketing*.

Right sourcing and highly efficient logistics becomes the key. The scale of operations also gives a company a distinct advantage.

5. How far can we go in customizing our offering for each customer?

   With a virtual warehouse, there are less limitations on making a complete range available to suit nearly all customers.

6. What are the major ways in which we can grow our business?

   Wider range, better quality, faster delivery, lower price, and fast response to problems are the keys to success in the new age.

7. How can we build stronger brands?

   If one does what has been listed above in question 6, the brand becomes stronger, for example, Amazon, from where customers buy books to consumer durables and shoes and clothing.

8. How can we reduce the cost of customer acquisition?

   It could be done with the use of finely tuned net advertising and social media, and highly personalized and focused customer service; we also benefit from word of mouth.

9. How can we keep our customers loyal for a longer period?

   A continued and relentless pursuit of the goals set out in question 6 is what will help finding answers for question 8 and 9.

10. How can we tell which customers are more important?

    Ongoing research is done by most of the pioneers and big companies in e-commerce and they know many of the answers. As a result, they focus on the

youth market—the gen-next—and also for the certain type of products on the Tier 2 & Tier 3 towns rather than the metros.
11. How can we measure the payback from advertising, sales promotion, and public relations?
Since a lot of expenditure is through social media, this is easier to direct, measure and to control. Computer tools now enable you to do this.
12. How can we improve sales force productivity?
This will always remain a challenge, but in e-commerce, the role of salesmen in direct selling to the customer is more restricted. However, in (b/m), we will use more technology to increase salesman knowledge levels, empower him, monitor him, and enable him to self-manage.
13. How can we establish multiple channels and yet manage channel conflict?
Many experiments are under way, especially in countries like India where they seek to marry e-commerce with b/m, and b/m retail outlets are used as the final warehouse for the e-commerce company. They seek to cooperate rather than to compete.
14. How can we get all the company departments to be more customers oriented?
In the e-commerce world, it may be easier to band the team together than in the traditional dispersed organization. But there are the commonalities— vision, goals, and unflagging customer orientation.

The above questions have been taken from the book *Marketing*, authored by Professor Philip Kotler. Some of these questions are less relevant in E-commerce and some more relevant and important. The whole area of "delivery" is critical in E-commerce, what with virtual warehousing of perhaps a million items (unthinkable, even ten years ago) offering a wider range of products, coupled with the increasing need for speed of delivery, where now even drones are used. The measurement of customer behavior and of advertising effectiveness is more accurate with the methods we have now developed on computers, like the use of big data and of cloud computing.

Therefore, innovators must ensure that their innovation fits into a real need, where the customer will find value in paying the price.

It is the ability to identify and remove customer pain points.

5

Add Width to Depth
Of Knowledge and Experience

The impatient manager cannot just be a specialist. Like any other traditional manager, he needs to go beyond "technical" skills to add "human" skills and develop "conceptual" skills. And do that at a faster rate than the others. The last one is the most difficult part. It is the ability to look at the big picture—the ability to go beyond marketing "hindsight" and to develop marketing "foresight."

Developing "width" of knowledge and experience needs wide reading, and observing real-life situations and learning from them. It means converting knowledge into wisdom. It is like knowing that tomato is a fruit—which is knowledge—but that it cannot be added to fruit salad—which is wisdom. It means developing the neglected skills which are taken for granted—faster reading speed with comprehension, involving correct and appropriate posture in interaction, ability to listen more than talking, and taking in more than what the words convey.

The impatient manager may sometimes not even have the "accepted qualifications" for what he is now attempting to do. We will find this from the lives of very successful managers like Bill Gates of Microsoft, who dropped out of college or Steve Jobs of Apple. It should be noted, however, that Gates also keeps advising young people not to emulate his example and that not all who opt out of college can fare as well as Gates did.

We find successful managers in India like Ratan Tata who did aeronautical engineering at Cornell University, USA, or Anand Mahindra, who did a course in filmmaking in New York. Even such seemingly unrelated learning added to their experience because with their width of knowledge and the depth of experience they later gained, they became driver, persuader, and teacher (DPT) managers. They are, like all the great managers and entrepreneurs:

> *Drivers*—who lead their people to achieve their vision,
> *Persuaders*—who can effectively communicate with those above, around, and below them, and
> *Teachers*—who can teach, correct, and motivate.

Even if the manager is not master of a subject—whether engineering or accounting—but is a DPT manager, he will succeed. If it is the other way round, one is not very sure of a guaranteed success.

KEY LESSONS IN LEADERSHIP: A CHANGING STYLE FOR A NEW WORLD

> *Building Marico would not have been possible if I had not focused on growth. And, I do not mean growth at the bottom line alone to the exclusion of everything else. I mean growth in a very holistic sense—where the organization grows, where the people in it grow, and where I grow.*

This is not to suggest that growth is the only metric to be measured. I place a premium on trust. By way of example, may I offer just one instance? At Marico, I did away with something as routine as people clocking in and out of work. Nobody has abused the system.

I must offer a word of caution here. I've had to watch out to the dangers of having people who nod "yes" to everything I say. Instead, I've learnt more from those who engaged me in constructive dialogues—even if that means rejecting an idea I come to the table with. I do not take offense to it.

I must confess this is not easy. It involves having to reinvent yourself constantly. That is why I keep telling myself I ought to be receptive to ideas and change. It does not matter who comes up with an idea or where it comes from. What matters is the quality.

Incidentally, good quality is a function of failing fast, failing early, having the humility to admit I failed, shake the dust off, and move on with life. In doing this, experience comes along as a mentor. It is the best teacher any human can have.

In doing all of this, I discovered agility is a good ally to have as well. Because, quite honestly, I don't have the patience in me to be locked into the paralysis by analysis. I'd much rather be on the move all the time.

Harsh Mariwala
Chairman, Marico Ltd.

THE STORY OF D.L. MOODY SANDBARS

A steamboat was stranded in the Mississippi River and the captain could not get it free. Eventually, a hard-looking fellow came on board and said:

"Captain, I understand you want a pilot to take you out of this difficulty?"

The captain said, "Are you a Pilot?"

"Well, they call me one."

"Do you know where the snags and sandbars are?"

"No, sir."

"Well, how do you expect to take me out of here if you don't know where the snags and sandbars are?

"I know where they ain't," was the reply.

Source: John W. Reed, compiler, 1100 illustrations from the Writings of D.L. Moody, Baker Book House

When one has the width and depth of knowledge, one is also able to connect and apply seemingly unrelated techniques from one industry to another.

WHO CAN BE A GOOD MANAGER?

The usual refrain in many companies today is that most of the unemployed are unemployable. They, sometimes, have poor technical knowledge even though they have graduated and even poorer communication skills and human skills. They have no hobbies. Their general knowledge leaves a lot to be desired. Yet, they all want to be "managers." "They do not realize that the person who knows 'how' will always get a job. But the person who knows 'why' will always be the boss—the manager." That is why only some, who graduate from college, will become managers and even fewer will become good managers, especially, if they follow the rules of good business etiquette as outlined by an expert, Letitia Baldridge.[1] She lists some behavioral traits that define a good manager, such as:

- Never expects others to follow rules which he himself does not follow.
- Makes time to listen to his subordinates and colleagues.
- Returns telephone calls/emails/sms immediately if possible or within 24 hours.
- Answers important mail within 4 days and other mail within 2 weeks.
- Does not pretend to be an expert on what he is not.
- Always returns borrowed property—like books or umbrella—promptly and in good condition.
- Never repeats a rumor that will hurt someone's reputation.
- Knows how to dress appropriately, both on the job and off the job.
- Answers all invitations promptly in writing or on phone.
- Is punctual, or if delayed, informs in advance that he will be late.
- Picks up the bill at a restaurant, when it is his turn, without being overtly miserly.

It may seem a big list. In fact, it is just what anyone who shows consideration for others will do.

---

[1] Letitia Baldridge in her book, *Complete Guide to Executive Manners.*

I have had the blessing of having worked for some very good managers who did much of the above. I have also been unfortunate to work under some impolite, incompetent, and highly political and selfish managers, who have taken the fun out of a job, even a job that I loved. I can see the shadow fall across their lives in their retirement. Prakash Tandon, former Chairman of Levers India, once told me, "You retire in the same way as you have lived." The selfish managers live lonely, cold lives and good managers are, most often, living warm and fulfilling lives with friends and well-wishers surrounding them.

DEVELOP YOUR OWN STYLE

Don't you sometimes wish to be as efficient or enterprising as your superior? In a quest to achieve just that, arises a tendency of one turning into a clone of his/her mentor/idol. The concept of "parallelism" is catching up rapidly today.

In management, we talk a great deal about ways to deal with the boss, the need to be guided by a mentor, the role of a role model in one's corporate life, and so on. With such a mindset, especially in one's young days, one is tempted to become a splitting image of the role model. In other words, one would unconsciously, perhaps, adopt the principle of "parallelism." If it is the boss who is being imitated then it might initially seem to be flattering to him/her. After some time, it may graduate into a mild or even serious irritation. And much later, it may create anger and be a source of jocular conversation for everyone around.

Superiors do not want assistants who have the same skills as they do. In fact, the boss would prefer assistants who have other skills. They want an assistant who will supplement their own knowledge and bring other skills to the table.

An ideal team requires thinkers, doers, and integrators. The thinkers will be few, the integrators fewer and the large majority will be of doers. If the boss is an integrator, he will not want a whole line up of integrators assisting him. He may need some, but he will need thinkers and doers in large numbers. Any attempt at parallelism by members of the team would be disastrous.

I was not very comfortable working with figures when I was pursuing my corporate life. And hence, I relied greatly on Venkat, one of my colleagues, who had a Masters in Mathematics and Statistics with an inclination toward mathematics. He pored over all the sales and profit figures, analyzed them, and produced reports which then could be interpreted easily and speedily by people like me. I did not need a "qualitative" oriented marketing assistant. I needed a "quantitative" oriented person. Any colleague wanting to work on a system of parallelism would not only be of little help but also would probably have been a liability.

Case Study

In developing "width" of knowledge, perhaps a key ingredient is "humility." The ability to recognize "what you do not know" instead of only proudly projecting what you do know. For me, a fine example was late Prakash Tandon, a Chartered Accountant, who rose to become the first Indian Chairman of Levers in India, later the Chairman of the State Trading Corporation at the PM's request, after that, the Chairman of Punjab National Bank and also of the Board of the Indian Institute of Management

Ahmedabad. An author and a speaker of repute, Tandon always carried a pocketbook and a pen. Whenever he heard a new or interesting idea, he always made a note unashamedly. Then he used this material in his own talks and writings. Talking of his humility, he has been seen—well after his retirement—taking an auto from the airport to his home. No chauffeur-driven cars for him anymore. Tandon stood tall and proud yet, he was humble of mind and spirit because he had a fund of knowledge, which, with age, he was able to convert into wisdom.

6

Go Beyond Technology
Add EQ and SQ to the IQ

In the fast movement toward the top or the pinnacle of success, one may forget the requirement of improving the Emotional Quotient (EQ) and Spiritual Quotient (SQ). Both of these are as necessary as high IQ to be successful. You will need the ability to understand other people above you, around you, and below you, and to connect with them.

Mother Teresa, a well-known social worker in Kolkata, later, a Nobel Prize winner, had once addressed a large national convention of personnel managers in Delhi, India, and compressed her keynote address into a few minutes by asking just two questions:

1. Do you know your people?
   Really know them, not just the obvious, but their hopes and aspirations, their fears and concerns and so on and their inner self as well?
2. Do you love them?
   In a very genuine way, do you have concern for their welfare and also concern for their families?

She believed this was the fulcrum of managing people in organizations, and if each manager in every organization did this, the world would be a much better place.

In an organization, you will need to build a genuine "connection." A concern for all the people you are associated with—customers, suppliers, and employees.

Case Study

My first job interview was with Ian Mckinnon, then Purchase Director of Glaxo India. I arrived to meet him on a very rainy day in Mumbai, with semi-wet clothes and a dripping umbrella. I was embarrassed but he put me at ease. He picked up my raincoat and hung it, ordered some hot coffee and talked about the weather. Before I knew it, we were already through a two and a half hour interview. He had put me so much at ease that I felt I had known him for a long time. Such was his EQ.

No wonder, some years later, he became the Managing Director, first in India and later in Glaxo, France.

Case Study

Many years later, I had another boss in another company, who was sent to a fortnight-long program on "Human Relations" at Harvard, USA. One of the rules he learned there was that you should always ask about an employee's family to establish a bonding. On his first day back in the office, he asked me, "How is the family?" I said they were fine and found it strange that he asked for the first time since I had joined the company two years earlier. When I met him later in the day, he asked me the same question twice. I was amused. He did not even realize or know that I was a bachelor, and had no family with me in that town.

This was EQ by "formula," and not by "heart."

Case Study

Look at the stories of Howard Schultz, the founder of Starbucks, who made Starbucks a star in a very short time. He looked after all his employees; even temporary hands were given full medical coverage so that they would never be in "need." Schultz was, therefore, not just admired, but also respected and loved. He went on to build one of the most iconic brands in the world.

Jeffrey Brotman and James Sinegal are the founders of Costco, the big wholesaler chain in the US, whose employees wear the Costco badge on their shirts with pride. On that badge, they carry the boast of how long they have been with the company—twenty years, twenty-five years, and so on—along with the baseline, "Proud to be at Costco!" The employees are so well looked after in their service conditions that most of them would not think of working for any other employer.

Case Study

Dini Gaitonde of Century Enka, India, a leading polyester fiber company, even as the President, went out of his way to help with school admissions for some of the employees' children and medical attention for some of those seriously ill, or even for members of their family. All of them knew Dini was always there. He spent as much time away from his desk as at the desk, yet the company grew in revenue and profit. The company morale was high.

EQ and SQ reinforce one another. SQ is not a formal religious quality. It is the sense of humanity, of belonging, and of subscribing to a core of ethics which goes beyond just "organized religion."

"A higher EQ and SQ enables you to evolve into a more 'complete' human being and takes you much beyond just a high IQ."

This helps to create balance so that there is reduced pride due to social progress and a reduced sense of superiority, which may come from money power.

A THOUGHT-PROVOKING STORY

YOU WILL BE ETERNALLY HAPPY!

A woodcutter had to struggle hard to earn two meals a day. He met a monk and explained his pitiable condition. The monk advised him, "Don't stop at the edge of the forest, go right in. One day's work will fetch you one month's food." The woodcutter followed the advice. Deep within the forest, he found sandalwood trees. He was very happy. He expressed his gratitude to the monk.

The monk advised him again, "Take the risk of going still deeper into the forest. A day's work will fetch you food for six months." This time, he found a silver mine. He thanked the monk again. The monk said, "If you trust me and go still deeper into the forest, one day's work will make you earn enough to fetch you food for a lifetime." This also turned out to be true, for he found a gold mine.

The woodcutter wondered why the monk still stays at the edge of the forest and not venture into the forest as he has been advising me. He expressed his doubts to the monk. The monk replied, "If you want to be eternally happy, sit under this tree and I will teach you to go within. Then you will be eternally happy."

To be an outer winner, one has to explore the outer world. To be an inner winner, one has to go within oneself. The balance between being an outer winner and being an inner winner is what would make us feel good.

Source: When Things Go Wrong, Inspirational Quote, May 2012.

WE DO NOT UNDERSTAND

Joy......until we face sorrow
Faith......until it is tested
Peace......until faced with conflict
Trust......until we are betrayed
Love......until it is lost
Hope......until confronted with doubts

Source: Author unknown, Cited in Lists to Live By, Multnomah Publishers, Inc.

Life is not a spectator sport... If you're going to spend your whole life in the grandstand just watching what goes on, in my opinion you're wasting your life.

Jackie Robinson (1919–1972),
Baseball player,
Bits & Pieces, August 10, 2000

DOES BEING ETHICAL PAY?

Many young people on the threshold of their working life mull over this question. They feel that there is a lot being talked and written about ethics—ethics in the business world, ethics in the political world, and ethics within the social circuit and in the family. They see that many of the people who have prospered are generally known to have been quite "unethical." Naturally, most of us want to progress and prosper. So what is the route that we should take?

I am reminded of a story of the preacher at Sunday service who gave a sermon to the congregation on following the straight and narrow path. In other words, the ethical way. He ended the sermon with the admonition, "And remember brothers and sisters, there will be no buying and selling in heaven." There came the loud rejoinder from one in the congregation from the back of the church, "That's not where business has gone anyways." There was a pregnant silence. The preacher was stunned. He carried on with the rest of the service in silence. The dissenter wanted to affirm that "business has gone to hell."

We read about the famous Mr Maddock who swindled so many people for so long with his "Ponzi" scheme and has now been sentenced to 150 years in prison.

There are thousands of finance advisors, financial dealers, bankers, and others who have used unethical means to make the quick buck and acquire large fortunes. In that process, they have tried to change Norman Vincent Peale's book title from *Think and Grow Rich* to *Cheat and Grow Rich*.

This is the time to reflect that the crooked path finally leads to disaster. It may take a short time as in the case of Harshad Mehta, the notorious stockbroker or a longer time as in the case of Ramalinga Raju, who is said to have misappropriated ₹7,000 crores or more from Satyam coffers, a company he founded. But finally, the chickens come home to roost.

Fortunately, there are some, among us, who have achieved great heights while still treading the straight and narrow path. For example, people who have achieved high office like President Kalam or who have achieved great financial success like Narayan Murthy, Nandan Nilenkani, Azim Premji, Vikram Lal, Harsh Mariwala, the Godrej family, and Kiran Mazumdar-Shaw. They have all achieved a modicum of Position, Money, Power (PMP), without resorting to chicanery or crime. They are all able to hold their heads high and look everyone straight in the eye.

One wishes the media would focus more on such icons who are models for the youth of India in the 21st century so that these candles may light many more candles, to make this a better community, a better country, and finally, a better world.

VALUES AND THE MANAGER

The best summary I have found, and practical to live with, is the one put forward by Cyrus Vance in his book, *Manager Today, Executive Tomorrow*. Vance gives eight basic attitudes, which I have expanded and elaborated on with my own thoughts.

From Birth to Death We Are Alone

There is no one in this entire world that can help us or be with us all the time during our entire lifetime. From birth to death, we are alone, only interspersed by periods of togetherness. That is why one must learn to enjoy one's own company to convert the concept of "loneliness" to a concept of "aloneness." Loneliness is negative, depressing, sorrowful, and stark. On the other hand, aloneness is positive, rejuvenating, and enjoyable.

This is one of the reasons why it is recommended that we all grow up from childhood with two hobbies—one collective, for example, team sports such as hockey or cricket, where you spend time in the company of others; and another creative, like music, art, where one can spend time with oneself.

There is a lot of sense in this guideline. It makes you less dependent on other people, on movies, TV programs, or video films.

No One in This Entire World Owes You Anything

We are all brought up to believe that people should do things for us. We all have expectations—some very high and some totally divorced from the reality. If anything is given to us, it should be graciously accepted. If it is denied to us, it is pointless getting annoyed. There are no rights or favors that are due to us.

Much of the unhappiness in the world today is not because people have lesser than the earlier generation but because expectations have changed and increased, and when these expectations are not met, people get annoyed and revolt.

The Word "Progress" Means Different Things to Different People

Most people measure their progress based on where they stand in relation to the friends who have perhaps gone places and are apparently very successful. Vance suggests that we measure progress by the objectives we have set ourselves in life and how far we have achieved these objectives.

There is little point in Arunachalam M—who refused to sell his technology outright and is still not a millionaire—the innovator of the low-cost sanitary pad making machine, comparing himself to another innovator, Sachin Bansal of Flipkart, whose 7.5 percent equity in the company he founded was worth $800 million as of 2014. Arunachalam helped 10,000 rural women by providing jobs of making pads and converted 3.5 million women in Asia and Africa to the use of the effective and more economical (₹2) sanitary pad. Each of these two men has followed his star and helped to make this a better world.

Never mind what other people are doing or have done. Let them do their own thing as you are doing yours. Let them follow their own star as you follow yours. Progress means different things to different people.

In Life You Accept That You Are Going to Win Some and Lose Some

Some people get spoilt as children because their parents give them everything they ask for—from ice cream to expensive toys. Later, they find it difficult to face a situation where they cannot get everything they want. It is the same with toppers in the school. They expect and get a pat on the back after every excellent performance in the exams. They expect that in real life, they will also be served "kudos" for their excellent performance. When they do not get it, they become despondent. They have lost the ability to fight for themselves. They expect the world to be fair and they also want to win every time.

The really complete person with a balance of IQ, EQ, and SQ faces up failure with some disappointment, but without the depression, bordering on wanting to commit suicide.

With Arunachalam's experiments on sanitary pads at home, first, his mother left the house in disgust. Then, his wife followed. He was left all alone. But he still pursued his dream and finally, after some years, he succeeded. He won many prizes for his achievement internationally. Fortunately, his family has returned now after his triumph. He went through agony because he had passion, he had a goal, and he had an unfaltering commitment to reach it. It took him seven years.

Like other managers/entrepreneurs, he knew that "in life, you win some and you lose some."

A Life Without Problems Is Impossible

Most of us are looking for a life which is ideal, where we will encounter total happiness and contentment without any cloud of sorrow. But this is a dream. It never happens. Perhaps, it happens in novels, in unrealistic movies, and in short stories, not in real life.

Look at the lives of our high-flying e-commerce entrepreneurs. Nearly all of them have failed once or twice before they saw success and became millionaires. Among many others, the same is true for Anirudh Sharma (Haptic shoe) and for H Satyanarayana (Virtual Trial rooms). They all know that life is always a graph of high and low points, of peaks and valleys. Some may have longer periods of peaks and for others; it may be the other way round. But we all have our due share of both, whether we are born rich or poor, intelligent or dull, handsome or ugly, brown or white.

No Matter What Others Say, You Never Stop Learning

At least seventy percent of the products we buy today were not available some twenty years ago. Impatient managers have made that happen and it continues to happen with more impatient managers coming on board.

This rule is not really applicable to the impatient manager because he would not be where he is, if he did not keep learning, questioning why it cannot be changed, or asked, why it cannot be improved.

As shown earlier in the book, impatient managers have quit jobs when they have stopped learning from their superiors, they have questioned the status quo, and found alternative solutions, be it cheap but effective sanitary napkins or Mitticool clay refrigerators, innovated by Prajapati.

Deepak Ravindran's offering of the offline internet on mobile phones through Innoz Technologies opened up a whole new world for 5 million people who use a simple phone which does not support internet connectivity out of 6 million people who have access to mobile phones. By connecting the unconnected, Innoz is changing the world for the better.

Change Is Taking Place All the Time, You Must Welcome It

Most people do not welcome change. They prefer the familiar, standard routine with everything in its place. I still visit the bank, although I could have done much of the work "online."

I selected a senior manager for a job in Mumbai with a forty percent increase in his emoluments from the present job and he turned it down because his wife would have to move to an upper class neighborhood where she would not feel comfortable.

It is only the positively oriented who welcome change and enjoy it, which includes the impatient managers as well. They do not wait for everyone else to change and then join in. They are among the first; they are the "agents of change." They realize that "the only permanent feature of life is change." The change also involves learning and relearning, which most of the people resent. But the agent of change does not resent it, in spite of the trouble involved.

"The impatient manager understands and accepts the fact that he must welcome change. In fact, he is a part of the change."

You Must Choose Optimism Instead of Pessimism

It is so easy to be pessimistic these days. The examination papers are leaked and sold. There is cheating at the exams. You cannot get admission into professional colleges even with a ninety percent score. Seats for "unreserved category" are very limited. Jobs are obtained only by influence. Fast progress in one's career needs a godfather. The country is going to the dogs. There is corruption everywhere. The old sense of ethical values has completely vanished. The prices of necessities are spiraling.

All this is enough to depress any normal human being, but it cannot be allowed to happen. As Henry Thoreau said, "Men were born to succeed, not to fail." A person with a positive attitude looks at the bright side of things and moves forward. He looks for ways and means to bring about changes and improve the environment. Instead of being totally influenced by others, he makes an effort to influence others. He keeps asking himself, "What can I do about it?"

These are eight basic values which will help the impatient manager to go through life as a "living" human being rather than being just a zombie. These basic values have helped me a great deal over the past many decades for which I am grateful to Vance.

TO THE "STATUS QUO ANTE"

Fifty years ago, I was hired by Glaxo India, as the first Management Trainee from an Indian University. Because of my qualifications in Pharmacy, I was earmarked for specialization in "marketing," an area not too well known at that time as compared to "sales."

After a few years, when I was made responsible for new product introductions, one of the products I had on-stream was a combination of Vitamin B1 and Vitamin B12. Glaxo was already a leader in Vitamin B1 injectable (Berin) and Vitamin B12 injectable (Macrabin). We found that many doctors around the country mixed the two and then injected the patient. So Glaxo developed a stable ready mix injectable to make it easy for doctors and called it Macraberin. The product was an instant hit. After just one year, Macraberin became one of the company's fastest growing products—a favorite with doctors and in turn, with chemists.

One day the blow struck. Over a period of four months, Glaxo received three complaints from different doctors in different parts of the country that a patient had a reaction to Macraberin. It was just three complaints out of the thousands of vials sold. It was known that the occasional patient is allergic to Vitamin B1. A patient could have got the reaction even if she were given just a Berin injection. But Joe Kidd, Managing Director of Glaxo, India, at that time would accept no explanations from the Medical Department of the company. He would certainly not accept any explanations from the Sales Department.

The manufacturing of Macraberin had to be stopped forthwith and the product was dropped from the list of offerings. No amount of arguments—that the number of complaints constituted 0.0001 percent of doses sold or that the patient would have gotten the reaction with any brand of Vitamin B1 or that this would imply a huge loss of future revenue, without any sound reason—could change Kidds' mind.

"Glaxo will always stand for ethical principles," he declared confidently. It was the time when Glaxo was Numero Uno in India. Kidd wanted Glaxo to be Numero Uno in integrity and ethics as well.

Fifty years later in 2011, we read a headline in the Wall Street Journal, "Glaxo settles with US for $3 billion." It had to settle several long-running criminal and civil investigations into the company, including allegations that Glaxo marketed some drugs illegally and defrauded the Medicaid program.

The settlement also covers a Department of Justice probe into Glaxo's development and marketing of the diabetes drug, Avandia, which has been linked to heart attack risks. The final settlement terms are still under negotiation. Andrew Witty, the CEO of Glaxo, says that this settlement

> is a significant step towards resolving difficult and long standing matters, which do not reflect the company we are today. In recent years we have fundamentally changed our procedures for compliance, marketing and selling in the US, to ensure that we operate with high standards of integrity and that we conduct our business openly and transparently.

Over fifty years, the wheel has turned full circle. And many may ask... Why did we put integrity and transparency to sleep for periods in between?

THE CHALLENGE OF AMORALITY

Perhaps the biggest challenge we face in India—and it would be true for many other parts of the world—is the challenge of "amorality." Many are losing the ability to distinguish between right and wrong, between black and white. It is all shades of gray. It would seem to follow the old dictum, "There is no right, there is no wrong, but thinking makes it so." If most people in the country feel like this and then act on such decisions, it will be like a ship without a compass—a sailing ship that sails whichever way the wind blows because it does not know where it is going. It can go anywhere.

The garage mechanic who repairs the car requested me to pay him the ₹7,000 I owe him by cash. "Won't a cheque do?" I asked him. He explained to me that he plans to buy a house in Mumbai and a house in Mumbai needs to be paid for with forty percent cash. So he was collecting the cash, not giving receipts so he can rustle up the forty percent that he needed to pay. He knew he was wrong, but justified his deed with the plea that he has no choice. It is a shade of gray, not black.

The medical doctor takes commissions from the pathology labs, from radiologists, and from consultants to whom he may refer patients. Is this a right thing to do? Is this system of commissions or kickbacks covered by a disclosure to patients? Certainly not!

A doctor explained to me that he has paid ₹60 lakhs to buy the premises for his dispensary. It is a lot of money in addition to the ₹15 lakhs that his education has cost him. Now the question is: how and when is he going to recover this large investment? Can he do this without a supplementary income from these commissions? Otherwise, he can only recover the investment by the time he is seventy-five.

The end justifies the means and again we have the shades of gray.

If you stand in the queue for the bus at Mumbai Flora Fountain, you will find that the queue dissolves as soon as the bus arrives. Then, it is free for all. The able-bodied push their way from the rear of the queue to the front. There is a little consideration for the elderly and for women. One of them told me that it takes two hours to reach his Andheri home from Flora Fountain and, therefore, there is no time for niceties and etiquette. He saw nothing wrong in what he does every evening as he muscles his way into the bus. He had become "amoral."

If this contagion spreads and if our young people are not imbued with a sense of morality in the home and in the school, India will one day collapse as a nation. A whole proud civilization would come to an end in the same way as earlier civilizations, like the Roman, came to a sorry end with a corrosion of the country's moral fiber.

PRIDE AND FOLLOW-UP

There are two areas where we generally fail in India. First, we fail to have "pride" in the work we do. It is seen in the detail. It is always the little things that demonstrate the pride people have in the work they do. It does not matter what the work is; it could be a manual work or it could be a mental work. The major job certainly gets done, but the small details are not attended to. And this reflects poorly on the author of the assignment.

Last week, the bus shelters in Mumbai were being changed. It was being done by the Brihanmumbai Electric Supply and Transport (BEST) at considerable expense. It is a new modern design with clean lines and, in fact, these have changed the ambience of the bus stops. But the workers have set these up and gone away without removing the paper cladding on the metal sheets—a cladding done to protect the material in transport.

Why did this happen? Lack of knowledge and moreover, lack of pride in a job well and completely done. Has this been noticed by anyone else? Perhaps not. Because it is unlikely that there is any system of follow-up either by the superior or any ombudsman.

Boundary walls at most places have a sign, "No painting or posters please." These are walls that look good with a coat of fresh white paint. Within days of the painting, slogans were painted on the walls by political parties or posters pasted by film companies. People ignore this and move on. Is there a follow-up to penalize the miscreants? None! Although there should be.

It is the same with the paver tiles laid on our pavements. Some of them have been fitted without enough foundation. The workers have pushed on, done the allotted pavement as fast as possible, and gone away. Many paver tiles have sunk in. They can cause grave damage to children and the old and can be the cause of falls, sprains, and fractures. Was there pride in the job? No! Was there a follow-up to evaluate excellence? Probably none or only superficial.

New speed breakers are set up regularly on many roads. A good concept, poorly executed. Many speed breakers are car breakers. They are too high and too pointed. They do not follow specifications. But is there a follow-up to the work done? Perhaps none.

There is a story of two bricklayers working on a project. When one was asked what he was doing, he said he was laying bricks. When another brick layer was asked, he said he was building the biggest temple in the country. Both were doing the same work, but one saw the big picture, a grand vision. He had pride in what he was doing. The other had blinkers on. He just saw the bricks. The famous author, Pearl S Buck, says, "The secret of joy in work is contained in one word—excellence. To know how to do something well is to enjoy it." If you have pride in what you do, you will always do it excellently. And if you do it excellently, you may not even need any external follow-up to check if the job was well done.

MAKING AND BREAKING OF REPUTATIONS

My friend and colleague Homi Bhabha told me that his father, who was one of the most reputed bankers of yore, kept dinning into the children that "there are only two things worth accumulating in life—education and reputation. Both of these cannot be stolen from you." Both take a long time to accumulate but can be easily and quickly lost. Here was a moneyman talking, and he did not put the emphasis on accumulating money. Homi told me that he, likewise, tries to instill these values in his children as well. Will they succeed in a world where established reputations are being broken every month, sometimes, every week?

In the recent times, there has been news about Mr Kahn, the French Minister who was tipped to be the next chief of the International Monetary Fund. He was accused by a hotel maid in New York and had to appear in court for improper behavior. He had risen in the hierarchy over many decades, and within a few weeks, he was a "hounded celebrity" both in the US and in France, in fact, throughout the world.

Another example taken is of Tiger Woods, an icon in the sports world and the uncrowned King of Golf. He has been caught out for infidelity, had a marital problem, which then affected his game, and moreover, his high reputation. It was a reputation he had built over a decade and it took just a few weeks to completely destroy it. The repair process has begun, but it is going to take a long time.

Maddock, the supremo of Ponzi schemes in the world, who became a billionaire, building castles for millions of people till it was found that these were the castles built on sand. He was finally caught and ended with a 150 years jail sentence, which can only mean "death in Jail" since he is well into his seventies.

Rajat Gupta, the brilliant and very personable young man, who won scholarships to work his way through IIT and Harvard and then joined McKinsey to become the first Asian to head the most reputed consultancy firm in the world. He even made it to the Indian Prime Minister Advisory Council and helped to set-up the Indian School of Business in Hyderabad. Finally, he was accused of insider trading and within a few months lost a reputation he had built over forty years, without money, influence or pedigree, but just by his own brilliance.

One is inclined to ask, what is it that makes intelligent, successful people like these, throw a dice and risk their solidly built reputation? Is it overconfidence? Is it arrogance? Is it the loss of judgment? One will never know the motivation.

It is enough to know that all of us have to be careful and to know that it takes decades to build a reputation and only a few hours to destroy the edifice so carefully built. It is like seeing the Taj Mahal on fire.

GONE FAR BUT NOT FAR ENOUGH

There has been a survey done which showed that in India the level of education is at 73 out of the 74 nations where the survey was conducted. The only one after us was a Central Asian country, which is a great shame. Has it not come as a surprise? We now have so many private schools from Montessori and the Tiny Tots chain to ICSE and the international baccalaureate schools, and with every worldwide connection you can think of. The stylish private schools also charge astronomical fees, totally out of sync with the earnings of the average middle-class Indian. And yet, where are we going wrong?

There are the large IT companies like TCS, Wipro, and Infosys which recruit 30,000 (and more) fresh recruits every year. They say that in spite of the large numbers of the unemployed, they find it difficult to find an adequate number that is employable. They have now gone beyond the IIMs and the IITs to graduate colleges in the metros, give them training and then put them on the job. They find that even this is not enough to get the large numbers. So they have gone further to the colleges in the smaller towns, like Pune, Coimbatore, and others to find a semblance of the talent they are looking for. Yes, there are many unemployed but most of them are unemployable.

It is not much different in the United States. Ed Gordon, a futurist specializing in education, and author of *Winning the Global Talent Showdown* says that it is a myth that the US does not have a talent shortage. In the past, this shortage was not very evident because the US brought in talent or they built factories in Germany, China, or India. But times have changed. People from China and India who came to the US for advanced degrees and stayed on to accept positions in the US are now returning home due to attractive business opportunities in their native countries.

According to Gordon's analysis of data from the Conference Board and Society for Human Resources Management, in the US alone, there are 5 million jobs that are vacant. Of these, 1 million jobs will not be filled because employers have given up either because the skills are too specialized or the costs are too high. Most of the vacant positions are in the science, technology, engineering, and mathematics (STEM).

This is also because of the big gap in the education system. In addition, students today are poorer than in the past even in communication skills—thanks to mobile phones, iPods, internet/email.

The *Wall Street Journal* says,

> According to research by three of the most respected research organizations—Harvard University, the Carnegie Foundation, and Stanford Research Institute—Technical skills and knowledge account for 15% of the reason you get a job, keep a job, and advance in a job. 85% of your job success is based on your communication/people skills.

Is it that both in the US and in India we are failing in the two important areas of STEM and CS? An urgent correction may be needed.

7

Build Networks
Most Often You Cannot Do It Alone

There have been times when people moved ahead alone. In the US, for instance, there are Henry Ford, Walt Disney, Howard Schultz, founder of Starbucks, and Sam Walton of Walmart; in Japan, founders of Sony and Toyota, in India, Jamshedji Tata and Dhirubhai Ambani, and Jack Ma in China. But often the impatient manager may find a faster route with a partner or partners. He has no time or patience. The IT revolution has helped this "not-to-wait-too-long" option to see the success of an idea.

IT'S MY BALL

It was Bijou Kurien, a doyen of the corporate management world in Kolkata and Mumbai, who first talked to me about the concept of "it's my ball." It was a concept that had given him grief time and again all through his professional career. Sure, I knew what he was talking about and I suppose most people do. A picture etched in our memory of our young days. It was one boy who owned the ball and another who owned the bat if it was cricket. If the boy owning the ball was out on the very first ball, he refused to leave the crease and all the others were accused. There was a tacit understanding. After all, he owned the ball. If he got out after completing twenty runs, he would plead to continue till he scored fifty. If he had scored a fifty, he wanted to stay on till seventy. In case others objected too much, he would just take the ball and go home. After all, "it's my ball." That was the end of the game and the end of entertainment for all of us.

This is a problem we face with many family-owned enterprises. The succession has to be within the family—a company started by the great grandfather or grandfather and passed on to the father and now to the son/daughter. There may be better qualified and experienced people in the company who can take over the assignment. They may even be aspiring for the CEO position, especially, since the family now owns less than twenty-five percent of the shareholding—though still the single largest shareholder. But the attitude continues to be of the neighborhood boy down the street, of "it's my ball."

Many years ago, the scion of the Boehringer family had to be "dethroned" by the board of directors of the company because he refused to step down in spite of many requests. The family, in any case, had a small shareholding at this stage and he could no longer claim "share power." But he had continued to use the attitude of "it's my ball" until it was shown that there were many other balls available to play with. There is a more recent case of Steve Jobs, who had to quit from the company he founded and paradoxically, also invited back to the same company to save it. The rest is history.

Surprisingly, this attitude is also a problem even in many professionally managed, widely held companies. Three decades ago, a large conglomerate found that it had "satraps" in their consumer, hotel, and chemicals businesses, and perhaps a few other companies. They were a law unto themselves because of their undoubtedly great contribution. Although they were just "executives on hire," they acted as if "it's their ball." "Take it away from me and the game is over" is what was left unsaid. Fortunately, a new group chairman had the courage to stand up against such "acquired rights" and bring them to their senses, to the benefit of the company and the shareholders.

More recently, the "it's my ball" attitude has permeated the field of politics. Membership of Parliament, of State Assemblies, and even of Municipal Corporations is sought to be passed on from father to son, whether in UP, Punjab, Haryana, or Tamil Nadu. If it is three generations, so much the better because the grip is greater. But even if it is two generations, it will do because the basic premise is that "it's my ball."

Bijou Kurien says that the "it's my ball" syndrome results in not playing by the rules as is understood and practiced by the rest of the world. It does make us think. Great institutions are not built and great lives are not lived on a foundation of selfishness and egotism based on the philosophy of "it's my ball."

"With the end of the over, the ball must go to the next bowler so that the game goes on and the team could win."

Having a partner or even partners helps the impatient manager to plug in and fill up other areas of expertise, which the main founder may not possess. Therefore, the warning of Mr Narayan Murthy in his message to young CEOs mentioned earlier. He followed this own advice when he founded Infosys and had partners who brought in other skills. He went further; each founding partner also took over the executive chairmanship of the company in the sequence of seniority so that everyone got a chance to be the number one.

From analyzing the background of many of the recent and successful e-commerce setups, one will see that most of them are partnerships rather than 'solo' achievements. They went together and hence, faster.

THE STORY OF THE TWO HORSES

Pulling Together

At a county fair, the townspeople held a horse-pulling contest.

The first-place horse ended up moving a sled weighing 4,500 pounds. The second-place finisher pulled 4,000 pounds.

The owners of the two horses decided to see what these horses could pull together. They hitched them up and found that the team could move 12,000 pounds.

By working separately, the two horses were good for only 9,000 pounds. When coupled, their synergism produced an added 3,000 pounds.

It's a hard lesson for us, but unity consistently produces greater results than individual endeavors. "Teamwork divides the effort and multiplies the effect."

Source: Bits & Pieces (Our Daily Bread), Cited in McHenry's Quips, Quotes & Other Notes, Hendrickson Publishers.

An Example

One of the finest examples I have seen in the recent times has been of Professor Philip Kotler, the world's high priest of marketing. He has collaborated with at least twenty marketing experts from right across the world—US, Europe, and Asia—to publish more than fifty books on marketing. These cover the entire gamut of marketing: from social marketing to marketing research, to marketing of art, and many other areas. It would have been impossible to do all this in one lifetime by one person. But by collaborating, he has been able to produce this voluminous output which has enriched the literature on a subject that has become so important in the new world.

On the other hand, Peter Drucker produced much lesser because he did not network in the writing of management books. He rode the lonely path and had a different style. To each his own!

THE PRICE OF AFFLUENCE

I was in San Jose in California, staying with my son, in a nice neighborhood, which had ten houses on each side of the road. Each of these was occupied by one family. Many of them were old California residents, who had lived in these homes for twenty-five to thirty-five years. One would have expected all of them to know each other and, at least, some of them to be "close and old friends." But does this happen? Unfortunately, no. They were all affluent and "private." Each of them minded their own business. They were only vaguely aware of the presence of the other nineteen and did not want to go any further. They preferred "aloneness" to casual camaraderie or even an occasional warm companionship.

Opposite to my son's house across the road lived two brothers—eighty-seven and eighty-five years old—both were single and retired from the Marines over thirty years ago. Unfortunately, the older one, Joe, went totally blind because of a misdiagnosis in 1986. George, therefore, did most of the outdoor work—shopping, city council, and bank—for the two of them. George was the "eyes" for Joe for twenty-five years. Yet, Joe made up for this by his prodigious memory. He could describe Nathan road in Hong Kong or the Taj Mahal hotel in Mumbai or the crossing of the Suez Canal or the Panama Canal with such vividness as if he had been there last week. But he was dipping into his memories of past forty years.

During my visit, there was a flurry of activities at 8 AM one morning. The fire brigade came in with the clanging of bells, followed by an ambulance, and parked across the road. We rushed across to find that George had died early that morning. They had come to take the body to the morgue. We were all shocked. We had met him the previous day and had a long chat. Although George had throat cancer and was being successfully treated, no one expected that the end would be so soon and so sudden.

When I came back to the house, I was surprised to see our neighbors on both sides, standing in their gardens. They were asking me—only a short-term visitor—what the commotion was all about. I told them what had happened. I asked them whether they would like to go across to visit Joe and offer condolences. One of them said yes with some hesitation because he knew him very slightly. The others said no because they did not know them at all. And that, after thirty years of being "neighbors."

Joe, now at eighty-six and blind will have to manage with house help or move into a "home." He cannot depend on neighbors because, really, there are none except as "physically present." The thought crossed my mind that the price of such affluence is the increase in privacy. The more affluent, the larger the garden and higher the compound wall. Even the builder, who lives down the road in

Mumbai, follows this guideline with a further addition of guards and a metal detector cabin.

The architect I met by chance at New York airport told me that the most unusual building he had designed was a hotel on a beach in Venezuela with 400 suites—each one with its own swimming pool. When I showed surprise, he said that this hotel was for the super-rich. At this level of affluence, they do not just deny dining in a common area, but they do not even want to swim in a common swimming pool.

Affluence takes one down the dark path of aloneness. In Joe's case, it is a truly dark path—both within and outside—in a world where you are no longer expected to be your "brother's keeper."

FEEDBACK BLOCKADE

Many years ago, in my green years, I was very impressed with the manner in which the Swiss Managing Director of Geigy, who was posted in India at that time, went about getting feedback. Every month he took off from Mumbai for five days and went to different parts of the country. On arrival—for example, in Hyderabad—he would hire a car and then travel for five days through Andhra Pradesh. He would stop at large towns and small villages checking out the availability of Geigy products at chemist counters, products that were unavailable, how often the representative visited, and when was the last time he visited.

He maintained a diary where all details were noted. The whole field force knew that the CEO made these visits diligently and with a focus. They made sure that the tour plan was followed and that the distribution of products was optimum. Geigy began to do well with a performance which shadowed that of much bigger rivals. It happened because there was "feedback" and it was direct feedback to the CEO—a feedback that was undiluted, unadulterated, and completely honest. He could then take actions wherever needed to correct the situation.

A bank in California has a system where the chairman and senior executives work for a few hours a week at the desk of the tellers, cashiers, and other bank staff who directly attend to customers. It serves two purposes: first, they get a feel of the reality of customer contact and second, this temporary substitution helps to motivate the general staff. No wonder the bank features in Tom Peters' list of companies "in search of excellence."

The Caliph of Baghdad knew, a century ago, the power of feedback. It is the power of what we now call "knowledge." He took time and trouble to go round the streets "incognito" to collect information which his courtiers would block from him because it was "unpalatable."

But most of us still refuse to learn the basic lessons. Our Ministers live in up-market areas where the roads have no pot holes. They seldom or never have water shortages or power cuts. They do not go to the market to buy provisions so they only read about inflation in the newspapers. They are received at the airports and walked to the waiting car so they do not encounter delay in getting their baggage—which sometimes takes half an hour or more—or beggars or touts pushing for hotels or the nameless who want to take care of your baggage to load onto the cab or the total chaos when you arrive at an international airport.

Our Chairmen and CEOs have seldom gone into the market alone and talked to primary (consumer) or secondary (retailer) customers. All their information is gleaned from the small coterie that surrounds them and who have made them captive. They live like Nero did, perhaps not quite but close enough, using or misusing the management concepts of hierarchy, delegation, job responsibilities, and so on to justify the arm's length approach.

Many of our problems in the government or in the corporate world are due to the feedback blockade—self-imposed. Will some of them break loose and breathe some fresh air? It will greatly help to solve some big problems with simple solutions.

ARE NETWORKS FOR EVER?

Networks, as partnerships, only sometimes last for a long time. In the case of Larsen and Toubro, one of India's premier engineering companies, the partnership lasted virtually a lifetime. But both partners wanted to call it quits and the company is now owned by public shareholders and part of the stock is owned by the employees.

In a few cases, the partnership lasted as long as the original partners. Then the children of the two partners begin to have differences and they then parted to have independent entities, which they can now well afford having a slice of the money got from the parent company. Unfortunately, many of these separations are acrimonious and leave a bad taste.

In some cases, somewhere along the way, the partners—especially in e-commerce, where success or failure come much faster—have separated and gone, each his way. They now had enough confidence, money, connections, and expertise to be "self-sufficient" and feel they do not really need each other any longer.

In other cases, they have got a good deal and sold like Sabeer Bhatia of "Hotmail" fame who collected $400 million many years ago and went on to do other things. Still, others have collected the money and become venture capitalists. There are still others who allowed themselves to be merged with a larger entity, like Myntra absorbed by Flipkart. They got an excellent deal and the founder of Myntra, Mukesh Bansal, also went on to work as a corporate manager in the larger entity and then quit after a time, perhaps, to embark on another startup. Such things happen quite often, for example, Taxi for Sure has been taken over by Ola Cabs.

"The impatient manager of today is different from the manager of old days." He achieves success in a shorter time, sees his dreams come true, derives a sense of achievement, and becomes a multimillionaire in the process, perhaps, before he is thirty-five. He then goes on to pursue another dream.

"Serial entrepreneurs" is a new term that has come into vogue in the last thirty years and is common, not only in Silicon Valley, but even in developing countries like India. Serial entrepreneurship has also been possible because the IT Industry cannot be controlled like b/m companies, which had to contend with a plethora of regulations: licenses to be obtained, red tape, and corruption from buying land to purchasing cement and negotiating electricity connections. In addition, there are labor laws that put you in a bind. Much of this is not applicable to the IT industry which, therefore, has wings and can fly.

NETWORKING: KEY TO SUCCESS

In a span of forty years in the business world, I have learned that sometimes it does not matter "what" you know, but "who" you know. In the 21st century, it is far more important than it was in times past. That is why it is useful for young people, even when they are still in college, to develop the spirit of "networking." The qualities of leadership, team working, and managing relationships will always come in handy in your life after school.

There are opportunities for networking in college. After that, there are opportunities for networking by joining the alumni associations of school and college. One can move further into joining professional associations like the management association or the engineers association or the consultants association. Or one can go further into joining social organizations like Rotary, Lions Club, or even Roundtable.

Times have now changed for the young compared to our days. Now you have LinkedIn based in America—an online business-networking website—as well as similar Xing based in Germany, and Viadeo based in France. You can now easily network without compulsorily attending weekly meetings and/or performing strange rituals. So LinkedIn, operating in 200 countries can most often be more effective for business contacts than a college reunion dinner. *The Economist* rightly says that while the old networks tended to be "clique-ish" the "old tie," the new online networks, by contrast, make companies and societies work better. They create links that cross national borders. They help people exchange information about each other's talents and businesses. They encourage the generation of new business ideas.

I believe that finally if you can combine the advantages of the old world network with the convenience and long reach of the new world network, you are bound for great success in your career in the 2000s.

Case Study

Look at the case of Vikram Gandhi who had a good academic record and when he was doing articles for Chartered Accountancy, was elected the world president of AISEC—the world organization of students of economics. He took a one-year break and went to Europe to AISEC headquarters and worked as the full-time President. It gave Vikram the exposure he could never have imagined. Working with students in fifty countries and managing a large organization in a foreign land honed all his skills in networking, team working, and of managing relationships. After he completed his CA, Vikram got admission in Harvard and never looked back after graduating. Today he is among the highest level executives in the financial world in New York and has now also started operations in New Delhi, India, to maintain a foothold in his native land.

Case Study

The late Ismail Merchant, from Mumbai, who later became a famous film producer-director in Hollywood, was a contemporary of mine at St Xavier's College, Mumbai. When he spent so much time with the Sangeet Mandal—the Hindi music society—and had the annual event, inviting most of the top stars in Bollywood at that time, I thought he was wasting energy and time and not concentrating enough on his studies. But the Sangeet Mandal gave him an opening to Bollywood which helped to open doors for him in Hollywood to later establish Merchant-Ivory Productions.

It is a story of having a passion, identifying goals early, networking to put talents together, understanding consumer needs, and working hard to achieve success.

8

Enthusiasm and Perseverance
Twin Engines of Success

ENTHUSIASM

"You've got to go out on a limb sometimes, because that's where the fruit is."
—**Will Rogers**

"Only those who will risk going too far can possibly find out how far one can go."
—**T.S. Elliot (1888–1965)**

UNSTOPPABLE

When a group of two hundred executives were asked what makes a person successful, eighty percent listed "enthusiasm" as the most important quality, more important than skill, training, and even experience.

Before water produces enough steam to power an engine, it must boil. The steam engine won't move a train an inch until the steam gauge registers 212 degrees. Likewise, the person without enthusiasm is trying to move the machinery of life with lukewarm water. Only one thing will happen—that person will stall.

A.B. Zu Tavern asserts that "enthusiasm is electricity in the battery." It's the vigor in the air. It's the warmth in the fire. It's the breath in all things alive. Successful people are enthusiastic about what they do. "Good work is never done in cold blood." He says, "Heat is needed to forge anything. Every great achievement is the story of a flaming heart."

You may have sufficient skills, training, and experience, but with "enthusiasm" added to these assets, you will be truly unstoppable.

It is said that there is nothing that can replace "enthusiasm." It is the basic "spark" that can start a fire and bring the whole house down. Enthusiasm is what sustains passion—the basic ingredient for a successful career as an entrepreneur or a corporate executive. Enthusiasm and passion also sustain perseverance.

PERSEVERANCE

> Behold the Turtle. He makes progress only when he sticks his neck out.
> *James B. Conant*

There is nothing better that can accompany "enthusiasm" than "perseverance." Enthusiasm without perseverance is sterile. Perseverance without vision, added with passion and enthusiasm, is like a motor car without a powerful engine.

Perseverance is a skill that anyone can learn not only to survive but also to thrive through life's curves when adversity strikes. It is not what happens to you, but how you respond to what happens to you, that have the greatest impact on your life. It is the commitment you make to yourself to do whatever is necessary to accomplish your dreams and goals. It means you refuse to give up in spite of the difficulties that surround you. It is the attitude that challenges you to say "why not" instead of "why." "Being persistent is the one thing which separates the winners from the losers."

> Dale Carnegie says, "Most of the important things in the world have been accomplished by people who have kept on trying when there seemed to be no hope at all."

It is passion, enthusiasm, and perseverance (PEP) that kept Edison's spirits up, even after failing with 10,000 experiments, until he developed the electric bulb.

Thomas Edison was born in 1857, and was an inventor who helped to change our world. Edison filed over 1,000 patents in his lifetime.

Edison is remembered most for his great invention of the electric light bulb. But most people do not realize that he also gave us the phonograph, the modern picture camera, an electric car, and electric power station.

Edison once said:

> During all those years of experimentation and research, I never once made a discovery. All my work was deductive, and the results I achieved were those of invention, pure and simple. I would construct a theory and work on its lines until I found it was untenable. I speak without exaggeration when I say that I have constructed 3,000 different theories in connection with the electric light, each one of them reasonable and apparently likely to be true. Yet only in two cases did my experiments prove the truth of my theory.

Significant Incident

It is PEP that kept Madame Curie focused on her work. Once, when she was invited to inaugurate a large sophisticated research laboratory in France, she was visibly upset with what she considered a great waste of money in constructing this impressive building. In her inaugural address, she opined that you need good people with good ideas and you need passion, enthusiasm, and perseverance to do great research. You do not need huge buildings. PEP is what she and her husband had in large measure while they worked in run down facilities. In spite of poor infrastructure, both of them made a significant contribution to the world of science and to the world.

There is a very long list of people who have had a dream, a vision, passion, enthusiasm, and perseverance. They have all become world-known figures but more than that, they have left the world a better place than when they came into it—the mark of a manager who changes lives to make it a better world.

There are many who have used vision, passion, and perseverance (VPP) to change the world they live in, for the better, even at the risk of repetition.

Dr V. Kurien, the masterminded of the "white revolution" in India, converted India from a milk importing country to a milk exporting country while improving the standard of living for thousands of cattle farmers across the state of Gujarat. He helped to make it a better world.

Dr M.S. Swaminathan initiated the "green revolution" in India and made India no longer dependent on foreign grain-aid. He changed the face of many states in the country that then became target segments for consumer and durable goods, especially in the northern states of India. He helped to make it a better world.

Bindeshwar Pathak started the first Shulabh toilets which were cheaper to construct, easy to maintain, and generated gas used as energy for generating electricity. He employed the former "soil carriers" as maintenance staff for the Shulabh toilets and extricated them from the difficult task they had been doing for generations as night soil carriers. He helped to make it a better world.

Case Study

There is a lesser known story of Chester Carlson, known as the Untiring Inventor.

The driving force behind an invention can simply be a strong desire to make a difference. The life of Chester Carlson proves it.

Carlson, the only child of an itinerant barber, used to work after school and on weekends as the chief support of his family. His father was crippled with arthritis and his mother died of tuberculosis when he was seventeen.

As a young man, Carlson worked as a patent analyzer for an electrical component maker, a job that required multiple copies of documents and drawings which he had to duplicate by hand. He thought of the idea of reproduction technique based on photo-conductivity.

Frustrated by the lack of time and suffering from painful attacks of arthritis, Carlson decided to dip into his meager savings to pursue his research. Carlson took his idea to more than 20 companies and they all turned him down. Even the National Inventors Council dismissed his work. Later he wrote, "Several times I decided to drop the idea completely. But each time I returned to try again. I was thoroughly convinced that the invention was too promising to be dormant."

After seven long years of rejections, a small company agreed to purchase the rights for his invention which developed into the Xerox Machine. The astounding success of xerography is all the more remarkable because it was given little hope of surviving its infancy. Today, xerography is the foundation stone of a gigantic worldwide copying industry.

Source: Inspirational Quotes, May 2012.

DEFEAT TO VICTORY

At the start of a career, we look at the world with rose-tinted glasses. Everything should go our way. After all, we may have tried very hard to get into college, then perhaps into a technical college (IIT?) then perhaps a management college (IIM?). All this takes a lot of time and effort. It means Common Admission Test (CAT) scores and Joint Entrance Examination (JEE) exams and perhaps coaching classes for both these exams. It means sacrificing leisure time, time with friends, time for sports or movies or even for TV. And then comes recruitment time, and students from even IIT and IIM find that there are not as many takers as in earlier years. And the salaries offered are fifty percent of those offered only a few years ago. The world economic meltdown is having its impact, which is quite disappointing and frustrating. It gives you a sense of helplessness. You have succeeded when the world has failed.

Even worse is what happened to my son in the US. During the summer at the management college, he was seconded to a large IT company. They were so happy with him that they made him promise that he will come back after graduation and join them. They offered an attractive package. They also prevailed upon him not to appear for any campus interviews. His campus interview was already over, they said. He had been selected. It was one month before he was to join—after a two-month vacation after graduation—that they informed him the Company was hit by the recession and they are, in fact, asking people to go. They would pay him three months compensation, but they cannot give him a job. He was there jobless. It was too late for quick alternatives. He had not appeared for any campus interviews. Now he was in a general pool of the unemployed with nowhere to go. He was jobless for three months before he got an acceptable assignment which was not the best. It was something better than nothing. But this experience made him tough. His later victories were perhaps due to such earlier defeats.

This came out very clearly at the ODI cricket match I watched on October 5, 2009, in Hyderabad between India and Australia. Here was Sachin Tendulkar crossing the 17,000 runs mark and setting a new record. He was playing one of his best innings. He scored 175 runs when India needed 351 runs to win. He single-handedly contributed half the required score. He also nurtured some of his partners at the crease like Raina. But at the end of the day, India lost by just 4 runs. Sachin had given an outstanding personal performance. He had supported and mentored in two outstanding partnerships. He had succeeded, but the Indian team had failed. Was Sachin a failure or a success in that match?

There will be times of defeat and times of victory with all of us. We all understand this. But it is more complex when we have a personal defeat in a group victory or even more depressing, personal victory like Sachin's in a group defeat. It can happen in any career—in the government sector, corporate life, a sports team, or even Bollywood, with an outstanding performance of the actor and film's failure. There can be the victory in defeat and defeat in a victory. Understanding this early in life will make us "tough" to face the world full of uncertainties.

A LESSON FROM THE DONKEY

One day a farmer's donkey fell into a well. The animal cried piteously for hours while the farmer tried to figure out what to do. Finally, he decided that the donkey is old and the well needs to be covered up anyway. So it is just not worth rescuing the donkey.

He invited his neighbors to come over and help him. They all grabbed shovels and began to shovel dirt into the well. The donkey cried horribly for some time when he realized that he was being buried alive.

Then, to everyone's amazement, he quieted down. The farmer looked down to see what had happened and he was astonished. With every shovel of dirt that hit his back, the donkey just shook it off and took a step up. The donkey did this again and again and again. Pretty soon, the donkey just stepped over the edge of the well and trotted off.

Morale: Life is going to shovel dirt on you, dirt of all kinds. The trick is to shake it off and take a step

> up. Each of our troubles is a stepping stone. We can get out of the deepest wells just by not stopping, never giving up.
>
> Five simple rules are derived from this story:
>
> 1. Free your heart from hatred
> 2. Free your mind from worries
> 3. Live simply
> 4. Give more
> 5. Expect less

> **BRIEF QUOTES**
>
> Sarasate, the famous Spanish violinist, was called a genius. "Genius!" he exclaimed. "For forty-five years I have practiced 14 hours a day. Now they call me a genius!"
>
> When Paderowski played before Queen Victoria, she exclaimed, "You are a genius!" "Ah! your Majesty," he replied, "perhaps, but before I was a genius, I was a drudge."

They say genius is ninety percent perspiration and ten percent inspiration. To achieve anything, a lot of practice is required. This drudgery is essential to improve yourself qualitatively. And while you practice, perseverance builds up stamina, ability, and character.

Enthusiasm along with perseverance can be used with a single focus, as it has been done by Madame Curie and Thomas Edison or by lesser mortals to change direction when they had hit a blank wall or found new opportunities. It will need the ability to learn, unlearn, and relearn.

LEARN, UNLEARN, RELEARN

It is now an exciting world full of opportunities, but you have to be nimble and move quickly to grab those opportunities. You also have to know what you can do and what you cannot. You have to further know what you could do if you retrained yourself to do the new things you need to or want to do.

The key to success in the 21st century is learn, unlearn, relearn (LUR). It is the essence of *The Fifth Discipline*, a popular book for managers by Peter Senge. Did he say something very new? Not exactly. He just highlighted what we already know, but might have forgotten.

In the formula LUR lies the key to changing careers, creating excitement, and moving on in life to do what you really want to do with passion and determination.

Case Study

Nikhil did his MBA at a business school in the US then worked with Citibank for three years in New York. After that, he got tired of the world of finance and banking. So what did he do? He liked the food business. He wanted to start a specialty restaurant in Mumbai in India, his hometown. He assessed that there would be a window open for Thai/Vietnamese food. So he went to Thailand and Vietnam and spent several months learning the art of cooking the two cuisines.

He came back to Mumbai and then began a catering service for parties. It was a premium service with food, crockery/cutlery, and bearers. It went on for some years and was a great success. He then graduated into starting his own restaurant, Busaba, at a premium location in Colaba, Mumbai.

Nikhil had changed direction. He had moved from banking to the food business. He had learnt, unlearnt, and relearned. It was not easy to switch channels, but he had discipline and passion to do so.

Case Study

I met Mohan on a flight from Mumbai to Chicago. By chance, he happened to be sitting next to me and as it happens on long flights, we started a conversation. This conversation kept me in rapt attention for a few hours when he told me his life story. Mohan was in the saffron clothes of a sadhu. He lived in Chicago. He had been in the US for twenty-four years. But, he was not always a sadhu.

He had done Electrical Engineering from IIT, Kharagpur. After that, he had immigrated to the US like most of his classmates. He joined a large Fortune 500 company and had a successful career as an electrical engineer. And then, he got a new idea. It happened that they could not get a Hindu priest for the thread ceremony of the son of a friend. Those that were listed were too busy. They were booked eight months in advance. Mohan, now single, thirty-one years old, looked at this as an opportunity to serve

> the community and also have adequate financial rewards.
>
> He is now a Hindu priest in Chicago. He resigned from his job, came to India, and trained in all the rituals over a period of two years. Then he donned his saffron robes and went back to Chicago. Mohan had been a priest for six years when I met him on the flight. He allowed me to glance at his diary; he was booked for functions for ten months in advance. His clients were from as far as Florida in the South to New Jersey in the East and from Silicon Valley to California in the West. His travel was all paid for and in addition, a handsome fee. He now earned much more than he did at a Fortune 500 company.
>
> Mohan had changed direction in a very unusual way. This, yet again shows that one can learn, unlearn, and relearn to tread new paths.

A career is not necessarily forever. Change is available for those who have discipline and passion, and to those who dare.

KEYS TO ENTREPRENEURSHIP

For nearly four decades, I have had an unquenchable thirst for stories which will tell me why highly successful entrepreneurs are successful. These stories are not easy to find because many of the heroes, I want information on, have died and so have most of their colleagues who knew them intimately. Stories that I look for are not the ones appearing in their biographies. As most of us know, biographies of the rich and famous are often tailored to meet the specifications of their families, friends, nonobjective admirers, and the needs and tastes of, perhaps, an undiscriminating public.

Yet, I managed to get a story about Jamshedji Tata, the founder of the Tata Group, from P.A. Narielwala, the former Chairman of Voltas and Ceat, whose father was a friend and colleague of Jamshedji. He recalled how Jamshedji often escaped from the city of Mumbai to the salubrious surroundings of Khandala for weekend picnics with his friends. They heard the constant refrain from Jamshedji on every trip, "Look at these waterfalls. If this was in Switzerland, they would have converted this energy into electricity." From this dream on his picnics, the vision of Tata Power was born. Tata was not just a dreamer; he was also an organizer and executor. He converted that dream into a reality with one of the earliest electric power companies in India.

When Jamshedji was refused admission to the classy Elphinstone Hotel—because nonwhites were not allowed—where he had been on an invitation by an English friend who was visiting, he vowed to build a hotel which will be much better than the Elphinstone and where all colors and communities will be allowed. Thus, the Taj Mahal Hotel came into the existence. Unfortunately, he did not live to see it open. From that single hotel, now it is a chain of over a hundred hotels all over the globe—the Indian hotels chain.

There was the less known, Walchand Hirachand, founder of the Walchand Group, one of the largest industrial groups in Western India with a whole township in Maharashtra—Walchandnagar—set up to manufacture heavy industrial machinery. Walchand started the first shipyard in India and the first airplane manufacturing factory. Both of them were nationalized during the Second World War to become Hindustan Shipyard in Vizag and Hindustan Aeronautics in Bangalore.

Walchand bid for the contract to build the Hirakud Dam in Bihar. After he submitted the bid, he went to meet Jagjivan Ram on a courtesy call. Jagjivan Ram, even in pre-independence India, was a Minister in the Local Self Government. He wished Walchand well and hoped that he will win the contract. Walchand said he was nearly certain he would. Jagjivan Ram thought it was "over confidence." When the bids were opened, a British company won the contract. But they had to hire all the labor from Walchand. Walchand had spent time and energy well in advance to hire every able-bodied adult for twenty miles around the proposed site on a two-year contract. It is rumored that Hindustan Construction made a neat pile on just the labor contract without having to make the big investment in the actual construction.

Ajit Gulabchand, the grandson, went on to narrate another story of Walchand. When he went to England to negotiate the purchase of engines for the planes he intended to manufacture, he was kept waiting to be seen in the reception area for two days and then told on the evening of the second day, he was asked to come after three months since the managing director was leaving for New York next morning. Most of us would have been angry and felt insulted and, perhaps, resolved never to do business with such an arrogant person who puts himself on such a high pedestal, but not Walchand. He found out the flight details and bought the seat next to the person who had not kept the appointment. They started a conversation and became well acquainted by the time they reached New York. And the man, who had kept him waiting for two days, signed the supply order and became a friend.

How do you describe people like Jamshedji Tata, Walchand Hirachand, G.D. Birla, Dhirubhai Ambani, and others like them who are made of sterner stuff?

They had the unique combination of conceptual skills, technical skills, and human skills. Whenever technical skills had to be bought, they knew where to buy, from whom, and at what prices.

When I think about these leaders of the industry, I connect with Donald Sull, who wrote a significant article in the *Harvard Business Review* of February 2009, on the two essential characteristics of great entrepreneurs—agility and absorption.

AGILITY has been characterized as "floating like a butterfly and stinging like a bee."

ABSORPTION was described as "taking a licking, and still keep kicking."

Donald Sull then applied these characteristics to two boxing legends of yesteryear. George Foreman was the reigning heavyweight champion of the time. He was a giant of a man. He had "absorption."

Challenging George Foreman was Mohamad Ali, who had "agility." It was the fight of the decade, held in Zaire in Africa with the whole world focused on what was labeled as the "Rumble of the Jungle." The prize for the winner was $10 million—a very large sum in those days.

Entrepreneurs, unfortunately, cannot be like boxers, focused on "absorption or agility." They need to have both these qualities. They need to fly like butterflies and sting like bees. They need to take a licking and keep kicking.

These qualities distinguished the founders of path breaking companies known worldwide—FedEx, Walt Disney, IBM, Siemens, Merck, and many others. It also distinguished the founders of giant companies in India, like Tatas, Birlas, Ambanis, Singhanias, and others.

"Absorption and agility" are the keys for entrepreneurs to venture and build the new enterprises for an awakened India.

9

Managing Jealousy and Envy
Killers from the Inside

This is the bane of the most lives. Most of us are looking over our shoulder to see what our friends or acquaintances are doing and how they are faring. If they are doing better, we are unhappy. If they are doing badly, we secretly revel in their unfortunate predicament. If they do well, we attribute this to luck. If we do well, we attribute it to talent. In this process, we waste a lot of time and energy and use up "mind space" on other people rather than on our own efforts, goals, and achievements.

Many years ago, when I was learning to sail, I was given some instructions by my coach, which are applicable to life as well. Forty years later, I have not forgotten them.

> Rule 1: *Focus on where* you are going. Don't look back or side to see where the others are. In that brief moment, you may lose control of your own boat and, therefore, lose an advantage.
> Rule 2: *Always be vigilant* for the current in the water and the direction/speed of the wind and keep adjusting the sails to be "in tandem."
> Rule 3: If you do both the above—*single minded pursuit of goals and put in intelligent effort*—you will win the race.

When I see so many young people in India doing this and building up organizations like Flipkart, Jabong, Snapdeal,

Quickr, Boxbe8, BookMyShow, Myntra, and thousands of others around the country, I feel gratified. They are all in the yacht race like real professionals and one can only wish them all the success.

Developing this attitude is not easy. It becomes easier when you have "passion" for what you do without caring about what anyone else would think or do. You just move on regardless. However, there can always be pressures from family, society, and community. It requires "single-mindedness" of purpose to get over all three and it requires confidence in yourself.

Case Study

I had a boss for whom corporate life and success were all that he lived for. He had no hobbies, no interests, and no skills except to work from morning to night, including the weekends. When I returned from the corporate office in Europe, with kudos for a presentation that I had made there on behalf of the company, he felt threatened. He felt that I may be eyeing his position and now I had built a sound base at the European headquarters. After I returned, our relations were never the same. He started bypassing me, giving instructions to my executives directly without keeping me informed, and in general, acting like an awkward child. I tried telling him that I had no designs on his CEO job, but to no avail. Finally, I quit to become an entrepreneur. It changed my whole life, as a result of that I evolved into a business columnist, an author, an international speaker, a visiting professor at business schools, and did things I would never have dreamed of.

> His jealousy opened many doors for me, or otherwise like him, I would have been a pensioner at sixty years, retired, and moved into the anonymous world, like thousands of others who then ride speedily into the sunset. Or at best, live through their children.

Case Study

My school friend (late) Kalyan Banerjee, who was my bench mate from middle school, made it big, faster, and better. He went to the London School of Economics, then joined a Bank, moved from the UK to India and rose to be the Chairman of the EXIM Bank of India. I was way behind such achievement in my own career.

We were always in touch. We met occasionally for lunch or dinner, visited each other's homes, but I had the nagging feeling that he had moved up and much higher. After retirement as the Chairman, Kalyan Banerjee joined the World Bank. On a trip to the USA, Kalyan insisted that my wife and I visit him in Washington and be his guests. We accepted his invitation and spent four memorable days with him—sightseeing, dining, and wining. I thanked the Almighty that Kalyan had done so well, remembered old friends, and shared his success with them. Was there room for jealousy and envy? Certainly no, just joy and gratitude!

When people do well and prosper and also take care of their fellow men, it reduces the possibilities of jealousy, envy, and anger within you.

Who will grudge Bill Gates for being the richest man in the world? Bill and Melinda have given much of their fortune for charities to improve the health of the poor, especially in developing countries. They have donated $27 billion out of $84.2 billion, that is, thirty-two percent of their total wealth.

Who will grudge Warren Buffet, the second richest in the world, the man who has contributed thirty-five percent of his wealth to the Bill & Melinda Gates Foundation, without even wanting to have another foundation in his own name? He has donated $21.5 billion out of $61 billion.

George Soros has donated 33 percent of his wealth of $24.4 billion, that is, $8 billion. The fourth richest man in the world, an Indian, Azim Premji of Wipro, has given fifty percent of his wealth of $15.9 billion, that is, $8 billion to reform the education system.

Who will grudge Narayan Murthy, who has given a large portion of his wealth toward the education of women in rural areas?

All these men and many others have gone on doing what they wanted to do, doing it well and succeeding.

They were not wasting their time on checking the position of other sailboats whether behind or alongside. They had their goals and they achieved them. Then they kept what they needed and gave the rest away to the people with greater needs. They, like many others, must have unwittingly countered jealousy and envy, but they did not let it bother them and cause any worry.

Jealousy and envy, like cancer, are silent killers of those who nurture them. It does not affect the person they are jealous of unless they have power over them, like my ex-boss. They are not even aware of the emotions they generate in others and go about their business as usual. It only kills those who harbor these emotions.

The impatient manager will have and should have no time or inclination to get into this "mindset."

> ### ANOTHER STORY
>
> I recently read the parable of the empty boat (source undisclosed), which I am sharing with the readers.
>
> A monk decided to meditate alone, away from his monastery. He took his boat out to the middle of the lake, moored it there, closed his eyes, and began his meditation. After a few hours of undisturbed silence, he suddenly felt the bump of another boat colliding with his own. With his eyes still closed, he sensed his anger rising, and by the time he opened his eyes, he was ready to scream at the boatman who dared disturb his meditation. But when he opened his eyes, he saw that it's an empty boat that had probably got untethered and floated to the middle of the lake.
>
> At that moment, the monk achieved self-realization and understands that the anger is within him; it merely needs the bump of an external object to provoke it out of him.
>
> From then on, whenever he comes across someone who irritates him or provokes him to anger, he reminds himself, "The other person is merely an empty boat. The anger is within me.

SIX WAYS TO KEEP JEALOUSY AT BAY

It may be worthwhile concluding with a reflection on "six different ways to keep Jealousy at bay" which appeared some time ago in the media. It is said that to be successful and contented in life, it is important to have a "sense of self-worth" and be secure in your achievements. It is also said that too much of the emotion of envy can have serious health implications.

Scott Bee of Cleveland Clinic says that "Secure people are the opposite of envious folks. When people are jealous they often over think and try to over control circumstances."

What are the six ways?

- *Surround yourself with trustworthy people.* If you are in a good company, your emotions are too. We are directly influenced by our environment.
- *Have a high sense of self-worth.* If you are comfortable with yourself and have high self-esteem, you won't feel envious of another person's circumstances or relationships.
- *Celebrate others' successes.* Whether junior, colleagues, or friends, the success of anyone of these does not mean you are failing.
- *Don't seek approval from other people.* In the book *Embracing Envy*, Josh Gressel dives into our desire to make others want what we have. This behavior is laced with insecurity. Such instant gratification will not last long.
- *Don't focus on labels.* Sometimes it is good to rid yourself of the usual trappings of success or status. You are more than your title or the awards on your shelf.
- *Don't compare yourself to others.* Ted Roosevelt says, "Comparison is the thief of joy." Just fixate on the positives in your life and theirs.

TO SURVIVE AND TO SUCCEED

After you finish your studies, and school and college are way behind you, then you realize that there is far more to life and success than just grades at exams. So you will find that those who were the top graders in college sometimes do poorly in the work-world and those who perhaps scraped through are the ones who shine. Why should this be so?

It is so because, in the real world of work, the great emphasis at the entry point and the lower rungs is on the technical skills. As one goes higher up the ladder, one needs to go beyond technical skills which are a "given." You need to have a large dose of human skills in addition. And then, there are those, perhaps only fifteen percent of the population in the company, who will have developed "conceptual skills." This is the ability to look at the whole picture, to have a "helicopter view." It's the ability to see how one decision will affect not just me or my department but the whole company and then perhaps the whole industry. These are the people who make it to the top—who are technical, human and conceptual skill (THC) managers. They finally become presidents and CEOs of companies. Of course, there may be some exceptions. There are those who got there by guile, deceit, fraud, or influence by climbing on the backs of others with spiked shoes. But these are still the exceptions.

Therefore, young people must know even before they venture into the work-world that there are six basic principles of business etiquette, which have been enunciated by Gary Yukl as the foundation for good human relations in corporations and in society. These six key etiquette rules will improve your business etiquette quotient and help you to get ahead in whatever job you do or aspire for. These rules benefit people at all levels—from administrative assistant to the manager to vice president to CEO—in all sizes of companies, whether a corporation of 50,000 employees to a self-owned business that you run from your home. These rules also apply beyond the corporate world to professionals like doctors, lawyers, and self-employed entrepreneurs.

And what are the six principles?

1. *Be on time.* Be punctual by sensibly scheduling appointments. It's the little things that add up. Show respect for other people's time and their own pre occupations.
2. *Be discreet.* So that you are sensitive to the impact that information might have on those working with it, as well as what the competition might do if they find it.
3. *Be courteous, pleasant and positive.* This is irrespective of the pressures on you or your company. Spread joy and cheer to lighten up the environment.
4. *Be concerned with others, not just yourself.* People's careers are ended, stalled, or reversed because they lacked concern for others.
5. *Dress appropriately.* First impressions are first impressions. You only make one. It is good to look, listen, and pick a role model. This always helps.
6. *Use proper written and spoken language.* Because people who can express themselves clearly are always at a definite advantage.

If one inculcates these rules in the behavior, even before entering the work force, it will be a great lead over the others in the race.

DO YOU NEED TO ACT RICH?

There is a big difference between "being rich" and "acting rich." It strikes me hard when I see strapping men with shirt's top buttons not done, displaying a hairy chest, and a heavy gold chain reaching down against the black background. It's black and gold. They also display, at least, two heavy rings on the fingers of each hand, sometimes three, and one of them has to be a *navratna* ring. It is the ring that brought the good luck, which brought the riches.

It is the same with some of the women as well. They are keen on showing off their dress, jewelry, and of course, the bag and the shoes. All items competing and clamoring to shout out, I am rich! Give me the attention I deserve! It has been said that most women can never have enough of all three—bags, shoes, and compliments.

All this seems unduly gross most of the times. How and when will people understand the value of understated elegance? No wonder Winston Churchill said that "It takes three generations to make a gentleman." And then I chanced to see this book by Thomas Stanley titled *Stop Acting Rich*.

Stanley conducted a survey of more than 1,500 people through the University of Georgia and found that more millionaires wear Seiko instead of Rolex or drive a Toyota instead of a BMW. Three times more millionaires live in modest homes in the US, valued at less than $300,000 than in homes that cost over $1 million. Warren Buffet, the second richest man in the world, lives in a modest home in a modest area and has been there for over two decades.

Buying brands is a frivolous idea nurtured by certain myths about a wealthy person's lifestyle. Much of this is cultivated and fanned by the media and the world of films. Generally, it is the not the rich who spend beyond their means and seek to buy luxuries in order to emulate the lifestyle of people who appear on TV or on magazine covers. Even the models who advertise these products or lend their name may not actually use the product or buy it.

Rich people tend to be frugal in spite of having the resources to splurge. Luckily we have many such examples in the past and even in the present. Some names readily come to mind, like that of Ramkrishna Bajaj and Soli Godrej. There is now Narayan Murthy and Azim Premji. These people and many others do not have to buy happiness through expensive toys. In fact, happiness in life has little to do with what you wear, eat, drink, or drive.

It would seem that the really rich and the really happy are those who pursue their hobbies, maybe playing golf, or interests in painting or in music or being involved in philanthropic causes or entertaining a few close friends, and so on rather than impulsively and continuously buying clothes (as Satyam's Raju did) or shoes (as Imelda Marcos did) or sports cars (as many maharajas of yore did).

It is, therefore, necessary to relook at our lives and our spendthrift ways and avoid getting trapped in symbolism. I was once told, forty years ago, by my English boss, "Walter, to live like a successful man, is half the way to success." I have thought about this advice often. If one did this, you may always remain at the halfway mark till the end of your life. It is unlikely that you will become truly wealthy if you keep spending in anticipation of becoming rich.

10

Never Forget Those Who Helped You on the Way Up
A Way to Connect and Care

It is a story that was sent on my smartphone by a friend. It touched me greatly. I thought I would share it with the readers through this book. It shows that those you help also in return help you and your personality in other ways.

> ### AN INTERESTING STORY (AMENDED)
>
> At the prodding of my friends, I am writing this story. My name is Mildred Honor and I am a former elementary school music teacher from Des Moines, Iowa. I have always supplemented my income by teaching piano lessons, something that I have done for over thirty years.
>
> During those years, I found that children have many levels of musical ability, and even though I never had the pleasure of having a prodigy, I have taught some very talented students. However, I have also had my share of "musically challenged" pupils—one such pupil being Robby. Robby was eleven years old when his mother—a single mom—dropped him off for his first piano lesson.

I prefer that students, especially boys, begin at an earlier age which I explained to Robby. But Robby said it was always his mother's dream to hear him play the piano. So I took him as a student. At the end of every weekly session, he would say "My mom's going to hear me play someday." But to me it seemed hopeless; he just did not have any inborn ability.

I only knew his mother from a distance as she dropped Robby off or waited in her aged car to pick him up. She always waved and smiled, but never dropped in.

Then one day, Robby stopped coming for his lessons. I thought of calling him, but assumed that because of his lack of ability he had decided to pursue something else. I was glad he had stopped coming as he was a bad advertisement for my teaching.

Several weeks later, I mailed a flyer for a recital to all the student's homes. To my surprise, Robby asked if he could be in the recital. I told him that the recital was for current pupils and since he had dropped out, he did not really qualify. He told me that his mother had been sick and unable to take him to piano classes, but that he had been practicing. "Please, Miss Honor, I just got to play," he insisted. I don't know what led me to allow him to play in the recital. Perhaps, it was his insistence or something inside me saying it will be alright.

The night of the recital came and the hall was packed. I put Robby last in the program, just before I come up and thank all the students and play the finishing piece. At that stage, I could salvage his poor performance through my curtain raiser.

The recital went off without a hitch. Students had been practicing, and it showed. Then, Robby came on the stage. His clothes were wrinkled and his hair was uncombed. "Why wasn't he dressed like other students?" I thought. Why did his mother, at least, not comb his hair for this special night?

Robby pulled out the piano bench and I was surprised when he announced that he will play Mozart Concerto No. 21 in C major. I was not prepared for what I heard next. His fingers were light on the keys; they even danced nimbly on the ivories. He went from pianissimo to fortissimo, from allegro to virtuoso. His suspended chords that Mozart demands were magnificent. Never had I heard it played so well by anyone of his age.

After six and a half minutes he ended in a grand crescendo and everyone was on their feet in wild applause.

Overcome in tears, I ran up on the stage and put my arms around Robby. I have never heard you play like that Robby. How did you do that?

Through the microphone Robby explained, "Miss Honor, you remember I told you that my mom was sick? Well, she had cancer and she died this morning. And, well... she was born deaf, so tonight was the first time she would have heard me play. I wanted to make it special."

There was not even one dry eye in the house that evening. As the people from Social Services led Robby from the stage to be placed under foster care, I noticed their eyes were red and puffy. I realized

> how much richer my life had been for taking Robby as a pupil.
>
> I also realized that he was the teacher and I was the pupil for he taught me the meaning of perseverance and love and believing in yourself, and maybe even taking a chance with someone and you don't know why.
>
> Robby was killed years later in the senseless bombing of the Alfred Murray Building in Oklahoma City in 1995.

So, many trivial interactions between two people present us with opportunities. Do we act with compassion or do we pass up that opportunity and leave the world a bit colder in the process?

> Imagine if trees gave free WiFi, we would all be planting like crazy. It's a pity they only give us the oxygen we breathe. So we do not perceive the "value."

The impatient manager will need a lot of help. Many times, it will be timely help that is required. And in his rush to the top, there will be those who let him overtake them on the road, who resisted the temptation to honk, who may even have stopped to help him when the car broke down or needed a tire change.

There is a good rule to remember: "Always be kind to the people you meet on your way up because they may be moving up on the escalator when you are on the way down."

Case Study

I still remember the late Parmeshwar, the Managing Director of *Reader's Digest* (RD), as if it was only yesterday. It was fifty years ago that I had finished as a management trainee and was executive assistant to the sales director, John Reece. I sat at a table in the general hall outside the sales director's cabin. Parmeshwar finished the meeting with my boss, came out, and introduced himself to me. Could he spend a few minutes to tell me about RD? Of course! I pulled out a chair and we had a chat. At the end, he said that I will get a copy with compliments from RD every month. He was the managing director and I was a junior executive, but he showed concern and care. I was touched!

Years later, when I had authority to choose media for advertising, RD was generally on the list for more reasons than the large circulation. I had never forgotten Param and his little courtesies and kindness.

Case Study

There was Sushil Kumar who was introduced to me as the new president of a large conglomerate in Thailand. I was invited to conduct a one day seminar for the senior managers of the group. I had a small chat with him over coffee before we could start. Then, Sushil was to inaugurate and give the opening remarks before I could start the Agenda for the day. What Sushil said came as a complete surprise to me.

He said in his speech that he had met Vieira fifteen years earlier, but I did not remember this. I had interviewed him for the position of CEO of an engineering company. I had spent time convincing him to wait for an opportunity where his chemical engineering background and his experience would be more appropriate. I would keep him in mind for such an opportunity in the future. He said that his attaining this present position as the president of the group was thanks to me. I had guided him right, and he was grateful for this.

I was so touched. It took courage and a certain uncommon honesty to relate this story. I shook his hand warmly after his talk. And then, I never saw him again for all these years. But the sweet memories remain, for him and for me.

Case Study

When I was a student at the university over fifty years ago, we were three friends who went for a picnic to the seaside in Juhu in Mumbai. In the evening when we were at the bus stand on our way home, there was a heavy and continuous downpour as only Mumbai can produce. We were wet, even standing at the bus stop. And then, a fancy car stopped and the driver offered a lift.

We got in, all wet and then I realized it was Naval Tata driving his Mercedes, and was kind enough to offer a lift to three dripping college students. I apologized for having ruined his car since I recognized him immediately—one of India's best known industrialists. "Where are you headed young men?" he asked. I told him he can drop us off anywhere on his way. "But where are you going?" he asked again. I told him we were going to the suburban railway station for a train to go home. He dropped us there. We must have taken him way out of his path, but we remember his kindness, even sixty years later. He projected the benevolent Tata image. Naval Tata was kind to strangers and students who were stranded and he had empathy.

Case Study

When Soli quit his job as the marketing director of the company and started his own consulting business, he also did a lot of work in the area of senior management recruitment. One of Soli's assistants was Khan, who had hoped to take Soli's assignment. In order to make sure that he got it, Khan kept whispering stories to the managing director and all the wrong Soli is supposed to have done when he was in the company. The managing director enjoyed this and was pleased, but finally, appointed another candidate from outside the company as Khan's boss much to his annoyance and disappointment. Soli had heard about the canards that were being spread by Khan from friends he still had in the company.

A few years later, when Khan applied for a senior assignment in another company, he was shocked

> to see that Soli was on the interviewing panel with the managing director of the company. He was so unnerved that the interview went badly and he knew he would not make it. And he didn't.
>
> Paths had crossed again. The chicks had come home to roost. Soli was again on his way up while Khan was on his way down. One never knows where life takes each one of us.

The earth revolves around the sun. This might upset a few out there, who still think that the world revolves around them!

> ### A TOUCHING STORY
>
> An elderly colored woman was stranded on the highway with the failure of her car. Many cars went whizzing past and she kept waving desperately asking for help but to no avail. To make the matter worse, it began raining and she was now all drenched.
>
> Finally, a young man stopped his car, asked where she was going, and offered to take her and her bags to the next town from where she could get a taxi to go to her destination. Not just that but he went further and got her a hot cup of coffee to counter the effect of the wet clothes and wished her farewell. She was so grateful that she had tears in her eyes.
>
> A month later, the courier brought a large box to be delivered to him. He saw it was a state of the art television set with a note stating: "Thank you so much, Ron.

> You were so kind to help me in a desperate situation. Thanks to you, I could spend the last two hours, with my ill husband before he died. If not for you it would not have been possible." The note was signed by Mrs King Cole.

POSITIVE HUMAN RELATIONS: A KEY TO SUCCESS

Someone was telling me a few months ago about his meeting with Bill Clinton. He met him for just ten minutes and said that Clinton has the ability to focus. He made Anil feel he was the only person who mattered when Bill spoke to him. His eyes did not wander. They were focused on Anil. He listened to Anil carefully and responded. He made Anil feel that he had known him a long time although this was their first meeting and perhaps the last. But Anil will never forget Bill Clinton and his kindness, his thoughtfulness, and his concern. Bill gave Anil a new sense of self-worth. The meeting increased his self-esteem.

Getting along with people is important in all walks of life but developing and maintaining good personal human relations in politics and in business is a must for a successful career. Andrew Sherwood wrote a book titled *Breakpoints* where he offers the following keys to good human relations. Of course, we all know these through experience, but it always helps to have a memory jogger in a properly structured manner.

- *Speak to people.* There is nothing as well received as a cheerful word of greeting. It is not just the words, good morning or good evening; it is also the tone, the look in the eyes, and the expression on the face.

It's the Bill Clinton style that makes you attractive to other people.

- *Smile at people.* Be generous with your smile. After all, it takes seventy-two muscles to frown and only fourteen to smile. Why do more exercise when you can get by with less? But again, the smile must come through your eyes, not just your lips. It has to be a "genuine" smile.
- *Call people by name.* The sweetest music to anyone's ears is the sound of his or her own name. And the less the person is a public figure and the less frequently you have met and yet you remember the name, the sweeter it sounds.
- *Be friendly and helpful.* Do unto others as you would have them do unto you. It can be even simple things like promising to give a telephone number next day of an old friend that someone wants to contact. One does not have to do big favors. In fact, these are not generally expected.
- *Be cordial.* Speak and act as if everything you do is a genuine pleasure, not an intrusion and certainly not a burden.
- *Be sincerely interested in people.* You can like everybody if you try. The trouble is we make up our minds about people in advance based on their looks, their dress, or what someone might have whispered into our ears.
- *Be generous with praise, cautious with criticism.* What you say always goes around and back to the person. You can make friends or enemies this way.
- *Be thoughtful of the opinion of others.* There are three sides to a controversy—yours, the other persons, and the right one. It is always best to state

your position and back off rather than persisting in holding the fort.
- *Be considerate for the feelings of others.* It will be appreciated. If you cannot find anything to say, they say nothing. Winston Churchill's advice holds true, "You must know when to stand up and speak out and also know when to sit down and shut up."

It's nothing new but bears constant reminding, if we are going to add a large dose of human skills to our technical skills.

11

Key Lessons in Leadership
A Changing Style for a New World

Leadership Alone Will Prepare You for Long Innings

Over the last four decades working in large organizations, I have learned some key lessons which I am happy to share with my young friends. Success can be our biggest enemy, and quick success can sometimes make us arrogant and reckless and, therefore, managing success is the key issue for everyone aspiring to have long innings in the career and business. So, also, learn to manage adversity. Resilience is a key to success.

It is extremely important to remain grounded in reality and critical to manage the "self." Personal awareness is another key to success. Managing relationship requires a deep understanding of the self in terms of one's nature, anxieties, motivations, angularities, strengths, and so on. A personal reflection about our behavior, outcomes, and relationships is the key to personal growth and leadership. A short cut is always a short cut and, therefore, the tendency to reach to the top in business or career through unscrupulous means is always fraught with risks

> which can destroy one forever. Therefore, work with patience and perseverance.
> Competence is not everything; it is the passion that delivers. Build passion in the team by creating space for personal growth for others. Leaders don't always hog the limelight, they allow others to shine as much.
> Finally, apart from tangible results in business, always work on developing intangibles like human resources, leadership, brand, ethical conduct, governance, and finally a reputation. This will survive you for generations. This is what I have practiced in my work life and achieved results.
>
> **Anil Khandelwal**
> Former Chairman and Managing Director,
> Bank of Baroda

There are many tomes written on leadership and one cannot cover everything on leadership, here, in one chapter. Leadership is the most difficult element to define but you can recognize it when you see it. Leaders come in all shapes and sizes. They can look as different from each other—from Mahatma Gandhi to Winston Churchill—in dress, appearance, and background. Yet, both were great leaders.

I remember an incident of Winston Churchill, who said to a group around him in the corridors of the UK Parliament, when Clement Atlee succeeded him as Prime Minister and Atlee had just passed by, "Beware of Atlee. He is a sheep in sheep's clothing."

Yet, they were both Prime Ministers. One was deified as their "leader" during the Second World War, but after the war when elections were held, Clement Atlee was elected the new Prime Minister, not Churchill. They were two different personalities, poles apart. One was Conservative, the other was Labor. But both became leaders.

It is the same with two such dissimilar leaders like Jawaharlal Nehru, erudite, urbane, elite, West-educated, and rich family background and his successor Lal Bahadur Shastri, small stature, rural background, and simple living.

What connected the two was a commitment to serve the country, to leave the world a better place than when they came into it. They were connected by a "vision" for the future of India and unquestioned personal integrity. There may have been many who disagreed with their style or their policies but no one would have questioned their "personal integrity." They were models of financial propriety—after Shastri died, they found there was not enough money in his bank account to pay his insurance policy.

Malcolm Gladwell, one of the finest writers on Management in the recent times—author of *The Tipping Point*—writes that leaders in the corporate world and entrepreneurs need three important qualities: openness, conscientiousness, and disagreeability.

Most of the people either have openness or conscientiousness. It is rare to find someone possessing both the qualities. Either they are so creative but poor at the implementation that they cannot taste success or they are hard workers without a spark of creativity. Founders of Walmart, of Disney, of Starbucks, of Costco, and many others had a balance of both. That is how they took these companies to the great heights as we can see them today.

And of course, we have the new breed with the same combination such as Flipkart, Ola, Uber, Myntra, Zomato, Housing.com, and many others.

But there is a third requirement which Gladwell adds and that is disagreeability. These entrepreneurs are able to go against the tide of public opinion. They do not look for consensus all the time. If they feel they are right, they go ahead irrespective of what the others think. Ingvar Kamprad of IKEA is one such man. He developed the concept of "Do It Yourself" (DIY) furniture, thus, reducing the cost of transport and labor substantially—a great boon in the post-war Europe. He had the openness to see a new need. He had the ability to be focused on implementing the idea and ensure that there is delivery. But, at one point he decided to shift the manufacturing to Poland to reduce costs and it was the height of the Cold war. He received some strong criticism from his countrymen and even others in Europe; nevertheless, he went ahead and came through with success. He could face disagreeability.

We gave the examples of many famous personalities who have changed the face of India, like V. Kurian, Dr Swaminathan, and Bindeshwar Pathak who also had these three qualities of openness, contentiousness, and disagreeability and deserve to be role models for the youth in the country.

I would also add the name of Mechai Viravaidya of Thailand who changed the face of that country as a social worker without using the authority of Government to control AIDS, generate employment, and increase hygiene. Each Asian country would do well to have, at least, one or more Mechais to help bring about the much-needed change.

DIMENSIONS OF A HEALTHY LEADER

Robert Rosen, author of *Grounded: How Leaders Stay Rooted in an Uncertain World*, uses the metaphor of a tree that stays grounded in a storm. He says that there are six dimensions (roots) to a healthy leader:

- *Physical health*: Being strong enough to cope with the pace of growth.
- *Emotional health*: Being self-aware and with resilience to bounce back.
- *Intellectual health*: Asking hard questions, being curious, learning, and adapting to change.
- *Social health*: Being authentic and building mutually nourishing relationships.
- *Vocational health*: Having a passion for success and a meaningful calling in life.
- *Spiritual health*: Where you have a higher purpose and a sense of being part of something bigger than yourself.

Rosen says that who you are (nature) is grounded in your roots and that in turn, will determine the kind of team and organization you will build. It applies to leaders at all levels, including CEOs because healthy leaders are open to feedback and developing their own skills. They are also able to build healthy executive teams because they unleash human energy.

According to Rosen, a healthy leader in the West is Fords Allan Mulally and another from the East is Kumar Mangalam Birla. He says that both of them are always curious, always learning, and unleashing human energy to seize opportunities and grow the business.

Leaders in professionally managed organizations evolve very naturally into healthy leaders given that the six dimensions are well-nurtured over a period of time. Generally, these leaders achieve greatness and have to prove that they deserve it.

Leaders in family managed businesses will find the evolution more difficult, but not impossible. They are to the "manor born." They have had a more protected environment. They did not have to earn every spur and take thirty years to do so. In this process, they are prone to be lacking in emotional health.

There is also the "danger of lack of social health," because they are in a position where many will fawn on them, try to be in the inner circle, ensure a regular diet of flattery, and all sometimes to a ridiculous extent. All this can also affect the spiritual health, where often the 1st can become the higher purpose.

LEADERSHIP IS EXAMPLE

There is so much being talked and written on the theory of leadership which includes different leadership styles of autocratic, democratic, laissez faire, participatory... the list goes on. But in all this jargon, many of us forget that leadership is about examples. What finally works and has always worked is "do as I do" rather than "do as I say."

In a career spanning forty years, I have been impressed by many leaders—and have been left unimpressed by many more—here are only two of them.

The first one is late Professor Madhu Dandavate, the well-known socialist leader of yesteryear and a Professor of Chemistry at Mumbai City College, who became the

Railways Minister. When Charan Singh government fell, he lost his job and came back to Mumbai. Once I saw him taking the train at Churchgate station to go to Dadar. It was just a week after he had been Railway Minister. I happened to be at the station and was surprised. I briefly met him and asked "why?" He knew what I had meant. He simply answered, "why not?" I had expected him to be in a chauffeur driven car, having been a Union Minister the previous week.

It reminded me of the photograph in the newspaper that I saw of Harold Macmillan, three days after he ceased to be the Prime Minister of the UK. He was at the bus stop, waiting for a bus, with a well-rolled umbrella in his hand.

Power had not corrupted either Dandavate or Macmillan. As Kipling had said in his poem "If", "You can walk with kings, without losing the common touch."

The second example that I am presenting here is of the owner (late) of Kwality Biscuits which was a big seller in the South. A large tea company offered to buy the company at a very attractive price. This was much before mergers and acquisitions became "de rigueur." Kwality agreed to sell provided his existing distributors and salesmen were allowed to remain in place for three years after the takeover. The buyer said no to this condition. The seller did not want to betray the people who had helped him build the company. After all, sales would only give him a personal benefit. Meanwhile, the staff came to know about this "failed negotiation" and was touched. Now they worked harder to make the company even more successful. Trust begets trust and one good turn deserves another. This was true, honest, sincere, and unselfish leadership.

There was J.R.D. Tata, Chairman of Tata Sons, at the door of the Shamiana restaurant at the Taj Hotel, which is a part of the Tata group. He was waiting for a table for himself and his two guests. On seeing them, the Manager immediately organized to set up a table for them since the hall was full and all tables were taken. But J.R.D. did not approve this. He insisted that the table should be given to the couple who were in the queue ahead of him, and he could be accommodated when another table will be free later, whenever that may be. Till then, he can wait. Diners sitting closer to the entrance were privy to all this drama and impressed that the chairman turned down what was offered to him, giving priority over other paying customers.

NUANCES OF POWER

Do you remember the story of the man who was working in his fields when the call came to defend ancient Rome against the invaders who were at the city gates? He left his ploughs and went to the city's defense. He took control, led the others, and motivated them to fight well. They won. The enemy was thrown back, defeated with many casualties. The leader went back to his fields and resumed the work he was doing before the battle. In today's management jargon, it is called the "situational leadership." It existed at the time of pre-imperial Rome; it exists today as well. It will exist in the future as we see it. It will remain "the best form of leadership."

He could have sought to remain in power and continue as leader/king after the battle and for the rest of his life. He did not. He knew what he wanted to do. He also knew what he had to do when an emergency arose and when the emergency was over.

"Power corrupts; absolute power corrupts absolutely" said Lord Astor. This dictum still holds truth.

Today, many of the problems in the government, in the corporate sector, and even in NGOs come from the corrupting influence of power. The wanting to get the right "Ministry" which is a resource generating one, the wanting to stay there indefinitely and create a fiefdom, and the remorse and anger when one is forced out leads to horse trading and selling oneself.

Power is sought to be captured and controlled by ensuring there is no ready successor. Many corporate captains have no excuse for not grooming one or even three possible successors in a ten or fifteen year period at the helm. This is a mark of poor leadership.

Fortunately, we have exceptions who prove the rule and can be great role models for future generations. K.V. Kamath of ICICI has put in place a succession plan which worked so smoothly that when he left it was not even noticed. Deepak Parekh of HDFC moved away but remained visible in wider fora, working out an excellent transition. Narayan Murthy put a succession process in place which has contributed toward making Infosys the powerhouse it is today. George Menezes of Hoechst was a pioneer in this context. Many years ago, he shifted his location to the training department and let his successor act as the personnel director for six months before Menezes' own retirement. Furthermore, he let the successor occupy the director's room before he was promoted.

For a truly excellent example of "transient power," one must look at the Jesuit order which runs institutions like St Xavier's. One among them becomes the Rector. He is the boss for two or three years. Then he reverts to the "ordinary." Another colleague becomes the boss and so it goes on. The boss has to be always fair as unfairness may be meted out to him when he becomes the "ordinary." Everyone knows that the position of power is transient. Young people need to reflect on power; not just how to acquire it but also how to use it and how to slip out of it with grace and without regret or anger.

LEADERS: THE "HALO" EFFECT

Sometime back there was a well-written article on the "halo" effect that is acquired by people when they become "leaders". The article suggests that people, after becoming leaders, attain a level of superiority over the general mass of the population as if they have been appointed by "the divine." They feel that they are above all and can do no wrong. All the hoi polio have to listen to them even if they talk drivel. They know they have the power, the money, and the status to do what they want, and they will do what they want to. In India, we are particularly prone to idolize those in power, whether Maharaja or Politician unlike the Scandinavian countries, who are at the other end of the spectrum in this regard.

In the political sphere, perhaps some leaders may get by with doing exactly what they want until they die or are overthrown. Those that managed till they died are the likes of Kemal Ataturk, Stalin, Mao Tse Tung, and our own Jawaharlal Nehru.

In the corporate world, it may generally not be possible to continue until death like country dictators. There are some checks and balances. There is, fortunately, the concept of retirement age which can be extended by at least five years. There is sometimes, more fortunately, the fixed-term of five years which can never be extended. There is the pressure from senior management to keep moving—otherwise the best people leave the company—so that space can be created at the top and in turn, space is created for middle management to top management.

But sometimes the "halo effect" remains—corporate leaders who will not give up power. They firmly believe they have been appointed by "destiny" to save the company. They believe they are irreplaceable and they must stay there for as long as they can. If some silly rules do not permit this, they will change nomenclature to the non-executive chairman, from advisor to the board, from senior advisor to the company, or any other designation that matches the "halo."

What are the characteristics that are common to "corporate leaders" who have the "halo" effect? I have tried to identify some of these:

- They believe they are "to the manor born." They are so convinced about this that it is contagiously transferred even to the mass of the employees.
- They have forgotten or prefer to forget the six most important words in Management of People, "I am sorry, I made a mistake." The leader never makes a mistake. His subordinates do and when they do, they are exiled.
- They firmly believe that "the boss is always right" is the rule no. 1 in the corporation. Rule no 2 refers to rule 1.
- They seldom ask the question, "What is your opinion?" These are the four most important words in the Management Inverted Triangle.
- And if they do, they seldom listen; really listen with wanting to learn. There is nothing that they do not know which is not worth knowing.

With all these traits, some corporate leaders create a "halo" effect that they have been the greatest gift to the company and unless they continue to give a helping hand, the corporation may sink and die. They honestly believe this, and the rest of us know that this is not really true. Corporations will live much longer than any high contributing CEO unless the CEO has made certain that they will both die together.

RATINGS OF LEADERS FROM STAFF: A RELIABLE INDEX

On September 2, 2015, the *Times of India* reported a survey done among the staff by US-based Glassdoor.com.

The highest approval ratings from employees was for the CEO of healthcare platform Practo Shasank Das (100 percent) followed by the CEO of Flipkart, Sachin Bansal (94 percent), Snapdeal CEO Kunal Bahl has the approval of ninety-one percent of reviewers, and Zomato's Deepinder Goyal received 88 percent.

Glassdoor makes the comment that companies with high ratings tend to have engaged and motivated employees, who believe in the company's vision, feel that their job matters, and feel they have career opportunities to advance within their organization. The employees also tend to share that they feel they get paid their market value, are heard by senior leaders, and enjoy some great benefits and perks too.

Among major IT companies in India, Infosys CEO, Vishal Sikka gets the highest at ninety-five percent followed by Cognizant's Francisco D'souza at ninety-four percent, and TCS, N. Chandrasekharan with eighty-seven percent.

In overall ratings of companies which look at parameters such as culture and values, work/life balance, senior management, compensation and benefits, and career opportunities, Flipkart scores 3.9 over Practo (3.5), Zomato (3.3), and Snapdeal (3.3). Among IT companies, Cognizant scores 3.5 followed by Infosys and TCS at 3.3 and Wipro and HCL at 3.1.

Such reviews say a lot about leadership, about top management, and about how a CEO casts a shadow across the whole organization.

LEADERSHIP AND INTEGRITY

Most of us expect that leaders would set an example of a high moral code. After all, the CEO casts a shadow over the whole organization and somehow influences most, if not all, who work in the company. Many times, the customers "image" of the company is derived from the perception of its products and its people, starting with the CEO. The way J.R.D. Tata conducted himself, created an image for the whole Tata Group even though he may have met a very small fraction of the number of people who worked for the group. This is true for all corporate leaders, whether past or present and is also true for leaders in all other fields.

This is why integrity and transparency are key elements in the make-up of any leader. This elicits "trust." It is a pity that some CEOs may not qualify on this score.

There are those who have started on the wrong foot. They have achieved the position by ruthlessly climbing on the backs of others with spiked shoes. There are those who have been compliant "yes men" and acolytes of the leader for many years. In one company, when the CEO was promoted to the Europe HQ as the head of South Asia; he chose his obedient acolyte to succeed him so that he could continue to run the Indian operations with a firm hand from Europe. Still, others in a family business may have been "to the manor born" and did not have to really qualify against set and accepted criteria.

There are those who have high integrity and solid values, but over time, have had these eroded after acquiring power and pelf. I knew a CEO who went from Mumbai to Patna for a two-day event to open the new depot of the company. He travelled by air, but had his Mercedes driven from Mumbai and back for use during the two-day stay. What an example of waste to the employees of the company. In a way, it was cheating the employees and shareholders with such displays of wanton extravagance.

Another corporate leader, who was unusually brilliant, led the multinational company to new heights of achievement. He had started as a clerk in the company and rapidly rose to be the CEO of the large multinational company. When the overseas headquarters (HQ) found that India was too small for his talents, they promoted him to manage all of the Asia from Singapore. Unfortunately, the higher he went, the lower his moral standards fell until the audit from HQs caught him red-handed with his hand in the till. He had slipped midway during a winning run.

There are corporate leaders who have a clean and successful run for a long time and slip at the time of retirement. A few "icons" of management have been shown to have "clandestinely" given themselves a large retirement moolah and, thus, lost the respect and goodwill that they had built over thirty years. They lost their integrity at the end of their careers.

Finally, there are those who have worked and retired with a clean slate—like Gupta of Mc Kinsey—and have been held up as role models for the youth of the country only to be tempted, past the active work life, to add some more to an already large kitty.

All this, of course, deals with "easily identifiable financial integrity." Putting the finger on the lack of intellectual or emotional integrity is far more difficult.

LEADERS FOR CAUSES

The media, whether print or electronic, is always full of sensational news—rape, murder, the investigations on Susairaj or Aarushi cases, the violence in Kashmir or Nandigram. There is so little on the positive side. There is so little news of all those people who do so much good, in their own quiet way, to benefit many in their immediate community and sometimes, even in the nation.

That is why I was happy to read the story in the *Times of India* of August 15, 2008, of a young man called Vikas Kurme who spends all his spare time promoting awareness about AIDS and spends one-fourth of his monthly income to finance the activities of his NGO—Sweekar. This has now grown into a large organization doing significant work in this area in Mumbai.

There is another report on a young man studying at Sydenham College in South Mumbai who travels all the way from Virar in the far north of Mumbai but after college spends all his spare time teaching young street children and help them to move on. People like Vikas are not from rich families. In fact, Vikas' father is a police inspector and he has two young sisters, but Vikas has a commitment to improve the world.

Again, on August 15, 2008, the *Economic Times* carried a supplement "Corporate Dossier" where top managers gave advice on how to improve India. Most of them did little, directly to improve the lot of the poor. Their companies did fulfill the "corporate social responsibility." They themselves perhaps can find a little time to get directly involved. In these articles, they bemoaned the fact that the political system was corrupt and inadequate to bring about "social equity." Yet, social equity is what all political parties are shouting about from the rooftops.

Who is going to change the political system? It will not change by writing articles. It will change when a large number of educated young people join political parties—any party they may choose—have voting rights at the party conclave and elect people like themselves to the positions within the party. Then, these people will select people like themselves for the legislatures and for parliament. That is how the whole political structure will improve. By keeping away and describing "politics is a dirty game" will not help to cleanse the system. We need to dirty our hands in order to clean the structure.

There are those who deserve high honors for continuously fighting against corruption and for the rights of the poor or the deprived or the persecuted. People like Anna Hazare, his son Prakash, and his wife Madakini Hazare, Medha Patkar, Bunker Roy, and others deserve the appellation of "heroes" of our time.

But all of us cannot devote all our time to fighting causes. It is enough if we can, at least, embark on a political affiliation and be active—not passive—participants. In the US, most people are either Republicans or Democrats. In the UK, they are Conservatives, Labor, or Liberal. They belong "somewhere." They participate in governance, maybe indirectly but effectively. Let us now do something that our parents perhaps did not do. Let us actively involve ourselves in the process of bringing about the change to build a better India.

TODAY'S LEADER IS HEALTHY, WEALTHY, AND WISE

Robert Rosen, a leadership expert, believes that to be a leader today, you have to be healthy, wealthy, and wise. He is the founder of Healthy Companies International and the author of *Grounded: How Leaders Stay Rooted in an Uncertain World*. The commonly held belief is that to become a better leader, you have to improve your performance at work. Rosen presents another point of view, "Who you are as a human being is what drives you at the work place and that will determine how well you perform." Rosen has spent two decades studying how to build better companies that balance results with the human side of business.

Rosen says that having studied leaders, he noticed two things. One is that the world is changing faster than the ability of leaders to reinvent themselves. Second, the model of leadership in the past was based on the paradigm that it is what you do as a leader that drives you as a person.

Rosen was featured in the "Corporate Dossier" of the *Times of India* of March 14, 2014. He says that the combined forces of competition, complexity, constant change, and information overload work together to box in the leader. His response to this crisis will determine how he and the company he runs will perform. This is where you need healthy leaders who are disciplined, self-aware, and committed to personal growth for self and for all those around them.

They are attuned to four agendas. The financial agenda ensures that they have the capital and results required for success and growth. The operations agenda focuses on efficiency and processes. The market agenda keeps them tuned to customers and competition. And the most important one is the human agenda.

It got me thinking about my client, the late Dini Gaitonde, who was the President of Century Enka—a highly successful B.K. Birla group company in the production of synthetic fiber. There used to be snide remarks about Dini spending more time out of the office than in the office. He used to go out to see employees in the hospital, to help with the admission of their children to better schools where "influence was important," to talk to specialist doctors about improved medical treatment for special problems of employees, and so on. Dini was a CEO who was not only admired but also loved.

One day he told me that he was surprised that the Chairman's son—Aditya Birla who ran his own clutch of highly successful companies—had phoned him to inform that he had met a very fine and personable young banker at one of his meetings and thought he would be a good match for Dini's daughter. Dini was touched that Aditya had the time and inclination in an altogether busy life to even think about Dini's daughter. Aditya offered to host a small party at his own home so the two families could meet. It was an enjoyable evening. The young couple liked each other and after a brief courtship, they were married.

It is the story of a man with who owned a multibillion dollar family business and had a human agenda as well, a story of a high-ranking professional manager who also had a human agenda, and the bonds that are created through genuine concern and caring to connect the two successful leaders even in turbulent times.

Finally, the essence of all leadership is 3Cs = C.

It is Competence + Connect + Care = Credibility.

12

The Corner Office Is Now Sometimes Temporary
So What Next?

"Ninety percent of those who fail are not actually defeated. They simply quit."
—**Paul J. Meyer**,
Entrepreneur and Writer

"Right now a moment of time is passing by... We must become that moment."
—**Paul Cezanne** (1839–1906),
Artist

WHAT DO YOU NEED TO SURVIVE IN THE CORNER OFFICE?

What you need to survive here is the same as what got you here in the first place.

- You need to have your VISION and use the ability to tell the story of how what you have done connects with what you want to do and get your team committed to this vision.
- You need to understand trends in the marketplace and constantly provide something that the world needs.
- You need to have the ability for objective self-analysis and understand your own strengths and weaknesses.

- You need to keep developing your learning agility. This agility will be more important than deep expertise.
- You need to be comfortable with uncertainty.

What you need to survive is to learn the nature of power and how it is employed. You need to realize that no one person can deal with the emerging and colliding tyrannies of speed, quality, customer satisfaction, innovation, diversity, and technology even if you are the founder. To realize that now, leadership is a verb, not a noun and that leadership is defined by what you do, not who you are. Thus, only those are leaders whom others follow.

Leaders, today, are expected to be essentially the same as they were yesterday, with attributes which have always distinguished the best leaders—intelligence, commitment, energy, the courage of conviction, and integrity. And, in today's world of the matrix organization and virtual leadership, one expects these qualities from just about everyone in the organization.

As Rousseau had said "man was born to succeed, not fail." Always be positive and you will succeed.

THE LONG ROAD TO SUCCESS

> *During the last forty-five years, I have worked for various large and global corporations. I have been a serial entrepreneur, and have run joint-ventures like Onward, Novell. I was fortunate to be a co-founder of NASSCOM—the premier body of the IT industry in India. I was involved in introducing a number of advanced technologies—some well before their time.*

From the travel on this long and winding route, I have learnt some lessons that I am sharing with my readers:

- *Life is a journey—an ongoing journey with only a "final end." So, do not think of retirement. Intermittent relaxation to recharge is acceptable. Otherwise, life should not have full stops.*
- *Take life seriously but not too seriously. That is the secret of equanimity. Remember that Nature's randomizer is at work 24×7.*
- *Have an attitude of learning. If you stop learning in the 21st century, you will soon be "brain dead," not medically.*
- *Develop methods to accelerate width and depths of learning across spheres, from faster reading to new technologies.*
- *Dream, dream, and dream! People like Jamshedji Tata earlier and Sachin and Binny Bansal now, all had dreams which they converted into reality.*
- *Have the vision and ambition to change the world a little bit with your efforts—to leave the world a better place than when you came into it.*
- *Be a risk taker. Of course, there will be failures. I have had my share. But, these are stepping stones to jump even higher.*
- *Remember that, especially in the services industry, high performance gets commoditized over time, if not continuously improved.*
- *Listen only to a few and preferably only the experts. But, finally listen to your inner self to take the final call.*

- Bring a team of like-minded and confident persons with diverse skills to meet the overall goal.
- Blend work, fun, and family and do not compartmentalize these too much. It is alright to have some over flow some times.

I still look back with satisfaction and look forward with hope. At your age, you should do likewise, perhaps, much, much more.

Harish Mehta
Chairman, Onward Technologies, India,
Ex-chairman/Co-founder,
NASSCOM, India

THE CORNER OFFICE CAN NOW BE "TEMPORARY"

In the old days, some of us finally arrived at the "corner office" and stayed there till retirement day. One could, therefore, be there for twenty years, like the Chairman of ITC or L&T, or for a few years, if he has arrived there very late and closer to retirement. Having arrived at the corner office, there used to be a sense of permanence which no longer exists.

HOW TIMES HAVE CHANGED

Look Back at Failures

One has to realize that the arrival at the corner office, either for the corporate executive or the entrepreneur, is bound to be after some failures. All the successes we see or hear about have arrived there after swimming in some rough waters.

METAPHOR OF LIFE

> Weather is a great metaphor for life—sometimes it's good, sometimes it's bad, and there's nothing much you can do about it but carry an umbrella or choose to dance in the rain.
>
> *Terri Guilemets*

At the ET Startup Awards in August 2015, the first prize went to Jaydeep Barman who, together with Kallol Banerjee, started Faasos which first started as a Quick Service Restaurant (QSR) in 2003 which failed. They then changed it to the first online restaurant. Faasos is now building one of India's fastest growing food technology brands. By the end of March 2016, Faasos expects to cover twenty cities across India. It is a case of "success after failure."

There were other contenders for the award as well. Ambarish Gupta started the cloud telephony company Knowlarity—after failing with his first startup—a real estate website called Inventica. Aditya Rao started LocalOye—a platform to help users find plumbers, electricians, or teachers—after his first startup Superchooha lasted for just a year. And Ritesh Agarwal started the successful OYO Rooms aggregating budget hotels, after failing with Oravel Stays for house owners to let out spare rooms on rent.

BEYOND THE CORNER OFFICE

From One Corner Office to Another

Your new company may be taken over by a larger company and the offer may be too good to resist.

Myntra, started in 2007 by Mukesh Bansal and two others, was acquired by Flipkart in 2014 for $300 million in the largest consolidation move in India's online retailing sector. Now, Mukesh Bansal moved to Flipkart and played an important role managing many verticals. They are now looking for a new CEO for Myntra. In the meantime, Mukesh has left Flipkart to write, perhaps, yet another success story.

CEO Shown the Door

Shareholders now often exercise their rights to oust CEOs for nonperformance and improper behavior. It has happened when Steve Jobs was asked to leave the company—a company that he had founded.

Another example in the recent past in the US is of Phaneesh Murthy of IGATE. He, too, was asked to step down because of inappropriate behavior. He took IGATE to the court and the matter was finally settled out of court with a payment of $4.6 million in damages to reach a settlement.

Heidi Stanley, CEO of Sterling Bank, said that she had been forced to quit because of her gender and her cancer diagnosis. She went to court and claimed $12 million in damages. The matter was finally settled out of court after 3 years.

In July 2015, the Board of Housing. com asked Rahul Yadav (twenty-six), a drop out from IIT-Bombay, co-founder and CEO of the company, to quit for "his behavior towards investors, media and the ecosystem, which was not befitting of a CEO." Yadav in his customary sarcastic manner reacted on his Facebook account, "CEO title of Housing. com. Take that away then what are you? Me: a Genius Billionaire (in INR) Philanthropist."

A Complete Sellout/Change Direction

Taxi for Sure, the company founded only in 2012 in Bangalore by A. Radhakrishna and G. Raghunandan, was acquired by Ola cabs for ₹200 million. And after exiting the venture, Radhakrishna is now an angel investor and taking his time to see what he can do next. Similarly, Phanindra Sama, co-founder of Red Bus, went away after being acquired by ibibo.

Reducing Control of Founders

A number of startup founders have diluted their stake to a minority, as a trade-off for boosting valuations. These founders are now worth millions of dollars. With stakes as low as twelve percent to one percent, they can be ousted whenever investor sentiment turns with lower than expected returns or any other valid reason.

Once again, it shows that the corner office is not as permanent as it used to be.

Corporate CEOs Have Gone Before Retirement

There have been so many changes in the corporate world with professional managers moving out well before the retirement age.

There have been changes at Yahoo, Microsoft, Vodafone, Deutsche Bank, and so many other companies in India and across the world. Boards of directors and vocal shareholders are no longer prepared to give the CEO multiple chances. He must perform or he must go. Many times, one feels sad that Wall Street dictates the decision, sometimes not giving the CEO enough time to ensure the long-term health of the company at the price of short-term gains.

On reflection, it would seem that the Hindustan Unilever model, followed for the last sixty years or more, may seem a relevant model where the chairman (CEO) serves a period of five years and no more, no matter how brilliant he may seem to be. It has worked well and smoothly for so long.

Not Forgetting Those Who Follow "Double Bottom Line"

The ET award for 2015 was won by Forus Health—one of the earliest hardware startups in India—a low-cost healthcare segment started by K. Chandrasekhar and Shyam Vasudeva Rao. It is a portable eye screening device called 3nethra to detect eye diseases early. Over five years, Forus has screened 800,000 eyes in twenty countries using 3nethra.

There are others, like YTS Solutions of Shweta Aprameya offering a range of financial products and services for SMEs, and NanoHealth of Manish Ranjan, which provides low-cost portable diagnostics kit, "Doc-in-a-Bag" for battling diseases in the slums.

All these and many others like them have refused offers from Investment companies in spite of the latter's persistent efforts. They believe that they are there for "more than money." They are there to offer a service, especially, for the under-served and the poor. Money and valuations are secondary, although they must have enough to sustain and to expand.

They work on a clear distinction between givers and takers, which is generally described as:

TAKERS VALUES

- Wealth (money, material possessions).
- Power (dominance, control over others).

- Pleasure (enjoying life).
- Winning (doing better than others).

GIVERS VALUES

- Helpfulness (working for the well-being of others).
- Responsibility (being dependable).
- Social Justice (caring for the disadvantaged).
- Compassion (responding to the needs of others).

A judicious balance of these values would make for a life well-lived.

ABSOLUTE POWER CORRUPTS ABSOLUTELY

This is a quote from Lord Acton of the UK which has been repeated so often that it has become synonymous with the subject of power.

Entrepreneurs, especially in the first generation, when they have total or majority ownership of the entity that they have founded, also have absolute power. Whether they use it with restraint, for their own good and the good of the community, or whether they misuse this power, is what distinguishes the "good" from the "evil."

An example of the latter is Ramalinga Raju, who was an early IT czar of India and was convicted on April 9, 2015, to seven years in jail and a fine of $1 million for an accounting fraud of $100 billion which caused a notional loss to investors of $200 billion and gave an unlawful gain to Raju and his partners in the crime of $30 billion. They were all convicted for criminal conspiracy, criminal breach of trust, cheating, using false documents, and falsification of accounts.

Raju had founded Satyam Computers in 1987 with twenty employees and when the scandal broke out in 2008, Satyam had 40,000 employees, 185 Fortune 500 clients, and operations in sixty-six countries. We still remember seeing him on TV receiving the E&Y Award for Entrepreneur of the Year, dressed immaculately for this black tie event and months before his confession in 2009, Satyam bagged the prestigious international corporate governance award.

But entrepreneurial success had changed Raju. He had an insatiable greed to own land. It is said that he had properties in sixty-three countries. This is how he siphoned off money from Satyam to buy more and more land, and when land values slumped, he was in a serious problem. He also got tempted to live a lavish lifestyle. He possessed 321 pairs of shoes, 310 belts, thirteen cars including Mercedes and BMW, and had a priceless telescope installed at his home.

Had Satyam been fully owned by Raju, there would have been less of a problem. But Satyam had got listed in 1992 and was oversubscribed seventeen times. A subsidiary, Satyam Infoway was listed on NASDAQ and traded at double of its face value on the first day. Satyam also followed with an ADR issue. After seeing this large flow of cash, Raju started fudging the books from 2001 and artificially increasing the share price. In 2006, Raju claimed Satyam had crossed the $1 billion mark in revenues. In the meantime, he reduced the promoters share in Satyam from eighty percent in 2001 to nearly zero percent in 2008. He made sure that only the unsuspecting investors lost.

The only good that came out of the scam is that the Government asked the Institute of Chartered Accountants and the Institute of Secretaries to probe the role of auditors and company secretaries. The focus also shifted to the role of audit firms—two partners were jailed and fined—and independent directors were also fined. The Companies Act was amended to ensure that such scams do not occur again.

A sad story of how a successful entrepreneur can climb to great heights and through gross indiscretion and greed, find his way to jail. Shades of Bernie Maddock!

The Future—Providing Egg Nest or Inheritance?

I have read about the accepted theory that each generation is expected to contribute toward building wall—a wall which past generations had begun building—until it becomes bigger and, perhaps, never completes for a long time. It presents shades of the "work in progress" of the Cathedral in Barcelona, which I saw being built twenty-five years ago and is still not complete. This is how great corporations of the past were built from generation to generation, for example, Fords, Agnellis, Cadburys, Waltons, Boehringers, Tatas, and Birlas. But, it seems that times are changing. Today, there are many families where the founders do not want to leave a legacy to their children. They want their children to start from the beginning and taste success or failure as the case may be. All that the progeny may inherit is the surname—for all that it may be worth. There are self-made millionaires and billionaires across various fields from rockstars to mayors, who want their children to have as normal a childhood as possible so that they learn the value of money and build their own careers and their own fortune.

Bill Gates, America's richest man, has directed a major chunk of his wealth of $78.9 billion to his fund for charity.

His children are expected to get only $10 million each as his legacy.

Warren Buffet, with $63 billion, has already pledged away ninety-nine percent of his fortune; and a lot of it has been donated to the Bill and Melinda Gates Foundation. He is reported to have said that he would provide for his kids "just enough so that they can do anything, but not so much that they feel like doing nothing."

Michael Bloomberg, politician and entrepreneur, with $34 billion nearly all of which will go to nonprofit organizations and charities across the globe. None of it will go to his kids or anyone else in the family. He says that "the best financial planning ends with bouncing the cheque to the undertaker."

Refrain of the old song "you can't take it with you!" It is the same with music composer Andrew Lloyd Webber ($1.2 billion), who will use his wealth to discover and nourish fresh talent, "to encourage the arts, rather than raise brats." Or George Lucas, the Star Wars film director with $5.2 billion who has warned his children that their inheritance will be meager. Or Ted Turner, the media tycoon, with $2.2 billion, who has already channeled millions of dollars to the UN Foundation and many more charities and the only money left for his family of five children will be for his own funeral expenses. It is the same with actor Jackie Chan ($140 million), musician Sting ($300 million), and even Nigella Lawson with a much less $150 million. Nigella Lawson that not having to earn money ruins children.

Will billionaire families in the East be influenced by this new trend in the West? In an environment where beyond business even elected political office is considered hereditary and an entitlement for the next generation, it may not be fertile ground for such new ideas. Not yet, at least!

A VUCA WORLD: A WORLD OF CHANGE!

In this VUCA (volatility, uncertainty, complexity, and ambiguity) world, everything is constantly changing. The CEO in the corner office cannot relax now that he has arrived. If he does, he may also have to depart as fast as he arrived.

In 1988, one in four beers sold in the US was a Budweiser. Now it is one in twelve. Between 1990 and 1999, Gap clothing sale grew double digit every year. Since 2004, sales have stalled. There are new kids on the block like from Spain, an unlikely source of world competition.

Blackberry (RIM) surged from $300 million in 2003 to $20 billion eight years later. By 2014, Blackberry had come down to $6.8 billion.

Nokia, which once ruled the world, tumbled down like Blackberry. It has now been bought by Microsoft. Sony, Panasonic, and some other household names from Japan have been pushed aside by Samsung and LG from the emerging powerhouse—South Korea.

Jason Jennings, a business consultant and author, says that nothing beats the elation of winning, of putting up big numbers, and leaving the competition in the dust. But success also makes risk-takers risk adverse, empowers bureaucracy, and motivates "yes men" to sweep any uncomfortable truth under the rug.

That is why high-speed companies follow the wisdom of Bejamin Franklin, "Doubt your own infallibility." Andy Grove of Intel advised, "Only the paranoid survive."

If we did the things we are capable of doing, we would literally astound ourselves.

Thomas Edison (1847–1931),
Inventor

Epilogue

Finally when all is said and done, the impatient manager in today's world must be the leader and yet, one of the team. He should be capable of managing:

- ATTENTION—to get others focused and motivated about the goal, also, making sure that he does not forget the goal himself.
- COMMUNICATION—so that he communicates the goal with efficiency, clarity, and urgency.
- TRUST—where people come to depend on you, and you are expected to be fair to them, irrespective of who they are and at whatever level.
- SELF—how one conducts himself in public and even in private, when no one is looking, and of assessing what one can do and where one needs help of experts in other fields.
- RELEVANCE—to customers, employees, community, and the environment.

In addition, if the business is built on a foundation of the twin pillars of "innovation and marketing," as prescribed by Peter Drucker, he would be an impatient yet successful manager.

AN APT SUMMARY FOR BUSINESS

Hari Menon, co-founder/CEO of Big Basket, an e-commerce company, summarizes the philosophy of his business in the new world, succinctly in the *Economics Times*, September 15, 2015:

> Just doing the right things gives you the best shot at creating an unbridgeable lead, create a culture that is a magnet for young people, sustain and nurture this culture continuously, obsess about your customers, customer trends, technology, and above all, build a strong foundation of values.

Goodbye and Good luck with a Farewell Message from the Blog of Adam Khoo, Singapore's Youngest Millionaire at Twenty-six Years

Some of you may already know that I travel round the region pretty frequently, having to visit and conduct seminars in Malaysia, Indonesia, Thailand, and China. I am in an airport almost every other week so I get to bump into many people who have attended my seminars or read my books.

Recently, someone came up to me on a plane to KL and looked rather shocked. He asked, "How come a millionaire like you is travelling economy?" My reply was "That's why I am a millionaire." He still looked pretty confused.

This again confirms that the greatest lie ever told about wealth (covered in my book, *Secrets of Self Made Millionaires*). Many have been brainwashed to think that millionaires have to wear Gucci, Hugo Boss, and Rolex, and sit in first class in air travel. This is why so many people never become rich, because the moment they have more money, they think it is only natural that they spend more, putting them back to square one.

The truth is that most self-made millionaires are frugal, and only spend on what is necessary and of value. That is why they are able to accumulate and multiply their wealth so much faster. Over the last seven years I have saved about eighty percent of my income, while today I save only about sixty percent (because I have my wife, mother in law, two kids, two maids, etc. to support). Still, it is way above most people who save ten percent of their income (if they are lucky). I refuse to buy a first class ticket or to buy a $300 shirt because I think it is a complete waste of money. However, I happily pay $1,300 to send my two-year-old daughter to Julia Gabriel Speech and Drama training without thinking twice.

When I joined YEO (Young Entrepreneurs Orgn) a few years ago, I discovered that those who were self-made thought like me. Many of them with net worth well over $5 million, travelled economy class and some even drove Toyotas and Nissans, not Audis, Mercs, BMWs.

I noticed that it was only those who never had to work hard to build their own wealth (there were also a few ministers' and tycoons' sons in the YEO), who spent like there was no tomorrow. Somehow, when you did not have to build everything from scratch, you do not really value money. This is precisely the reason why a family's wealth (no matter how much) rarely lasts past the third generation. Thank God, my rich dad foresaw this terrible possibility and refused to give me a cent to start my business.

Then some people ask me, "What is the point in making so much money if you don't enjoy it?" The thing is that I don't really find happiness in buying branded clothes, jewelry or sitting in first class. Even if buying something makes me happy it is only for a while, it does not last. Material happiness never lasts; it just gives you a quick fix. After a while, you feel lousy again, and have to buy the next thing which you think will make you happy. I always think that if you need material things to make you happy, then you live a pretty sad and unfulfilled life.

Instead, what makes me happy is when I see my children laughing and playing and learning so fast. What makes me happy is when I see my companies and my trainers reaching more and more people every year in many more countries. What makes me happy is when I read all the emails about how my books and seminars have touched and inspired someone's life. What makes me really happy is reading all your wonderful posts about how this blog is inspiring you. This happiness makes me feel really good for a long time, much more than what a Rolex would do for me.

I think the point I want to put across is that happiness must come from doing your life's work (be it teaching, designing, trading, winning tournaments, etc.) and the money that comes is only a by-product.

About the Author

Walter Vieira is the President of Marketing Advisory Services Group, Mumbai, India, which he founded in 1975. Prior to that, he spent fourteen years working with various corporations—Glaxo, Warner Lambert, and the Boots Company. A Certified Management Consultant (CMC) and a Fellow of the Institute of Management Consultants of India (FIMC), he provides training services and consultancy in business and marketing strategies to several organizations in India and abroad.

Walter Vieira has taught at leading management institutes in India—Bajaj Institute, Mumbai and ASCI, Hyderabad—and has lectured at business schools—Kellogg, Drexel, Cornell, Rady, URI, Lake Forest, NYU, among others, all in the USA; Boston Management School, Zaragoza, Spain; and other business schools in Thailand, Hong Kong, Nigeria, and so on.

He has published more than nine hundred articles in the business and general press and was on the Advisory Board of the *Journal of Management Consultants*, USA. Walter Vieira has also authored fourteen books, of which three were written jointly with C. Northcote Parkinson and M.K. Rustomji. His most recent books include *The Winning Manager* and *Successful Selling*.

He has addressed the World Congress of Management Consultants in Rome (1993), Yokohama (1996), and Berlin (1999) and the World Marketing Summit in Dhaka (2012), Tokyo (2014).

He has been active in social marketing for organizations such as Cancer Aid, World Wildlife Fund, and Consumer Education and Research Society. He is presently Chairman of the CERS, India and Trustee, MoneyLife Foundation, and IDOBRO.

Walter Vieira has served as the President of the Institute of Management Consultants of India (1987–92), was the Founder Chairman of the Asia-Pacific Conference of Management Consultants (1989–90), and Chairman of the International Council of Management Consulting Institutes, USA (World apex body) (1997–99).

Walter was awarded the Lifetime Achievement Award for Management Consulting in 2005 and for Marketing in 2009.